KWIK·SEW®
METHOD
SEW for TODDLERS
by Kerstin Martensson

about the author

SEW FOR TODDLERS is the eleventh of a series of books on home sewing by Kerstin Martensson. Her previous best selling books have achieved world-wide success and popularity. The overwhelming acceptance of Kerstin Martensson's books can be attributed to their illustrated, easy-to-follow, step-by-step procedures. Over a million copies of her books have been sold thus far. Many of these are being used by schools and colleges throughout the western world as sewing textbooks.

Kerstin Martensson is the President of KWIK SEW Pattern Co., Inc., and is internationally known as one of the foremost home economists. Kerstin was born in Gothenburg, Sweden and educated in both Sweden and England. She specialized in clothing construction, pattern design and fashion.

Kerstin has traveled extensively through the United States, Canada, Australia, England and the Scandinavian countries lecturing on her techniques to make sewing faster, easier and more fun.

Kerstin founded KWIK SEW Pattern Co., Inc., in 1968 to make patterns for stretch fabric as at that time none of the established pattern companies had patterns for this type of fabric. The company has grown into a world-wide operation with subsidiaries or offices in Australia, Canada and Europe. There are over eight hundred patterns in the KWIK SEW pattern line and the line now includes patterns for all types of fabric.

KWIK SEW Pattern company's growth has been credited to the patterns easy construction methods which enable the sewer to make professional looking garments in the least amount of time. The customers have come to depend on KWIK SEW for great fit and styling. All the patterns are multi-sized and have four or five sizes in each pattern. KWIK SEW has the largest and best selection of patterns for babies, toddlers, boys and girls. The newest addition to the KWIK SEW pattern line are Kwik Serge patterns which are especially designed for the serger (overlock) machine and they can be made completely on the serger. All these patterns have dual instructions for both the standard and the serger (overlock) machines.

Kerstin is encouraged by her customers' overwhelming response to her patterns and books, and she is dedicated to bringing the most up-to-date fashion and sewing techniques to the home sewer.

introduction

SEWING FOR TODDLERS can be a very rewarding experience, as at this age they usually do not have very definite ideas of what their clothes should look like and you can dress them as you wish. When they get a little older, they will want to dress like their friends and they do not want to look different. In addition to the fun in sewing toddler's clothes, you will also save a great deal of money as children's clothes are very expensive. At this age, children grow very rapidly and are constantly growing out of their clothes. By sewing the clothes yourself, you can allow for hems which can be let down and straps which can be lengthened. Another advantage of sewing the clothes yourself is that you can personalize the garment with initials, numbers, or appliques, etc. For example, a little girl looks very attractive in a pretty dress with a ribbon of the same fabric in her hair.

If you would like your child to appear to have a lot of different outfits at a minimum expense, choose one or two basic solid colors, which match each other and use coordinating colors for the other garments. This gives you the opportunity to mix and match all the garments. Each time you change the child's clothes, it will look like an entirely new outfit.

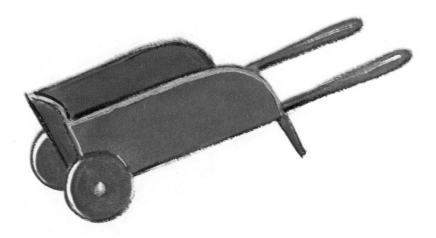

contents

SECTION I   GENERAL SEWING INFORMATION 9
Bias Tape. 20
Buttons and Buttonholes 24
Cutting 14
Hemming. 21
Patterns. 11
Pressing. 22
Sewing 17
Snaps 24
Thread 16

SECTION II   T-SHIRTS, SHIRTS, SWEATERS
AND BLOUSES 25
Front Tab Shirt. 37
Full Front Opening 42
Rugby Shirt 33
Cuffs with Button & Buttonholes . . .36
Sweaters 45
Buttons & Buttonholes. 49
T-Shirt 26
Fake Opening. 32
Ribbing Neckband with Ruffled Edge. 29
Snaps at Shoulder 30

SECTION III JUMPSUITS, COVERALLS, OVERALLS,
SLACKS, AND SHORTS FOR KNIT
FABRICS 51
Coveralls 60
Coveralls with Facing. 60
Coveralls Finished with Bias Tape. . .63
Jumpsuits 51
Elastic at Back Waist 54
Inside Leg Seams without Snaps. . . .56
Inside Leg Seams with Snaps 57
Jumpsuit Variations. 58
Neckband 58
Side Tabs. 59
Knit Pull-on Pants & Shorts. 67
Overalls 64

OVERALLS, SLACKS, AND SHORTS
FOR NON-STRETCH FABRIC 69
Overalls. 69
Overalls Square Bib 75
Ruffles for Shoulder Straps 78
Pull-on Pants 79
Pull-on Pants with Elastic around
Waist. 80

SECTION IV DRESSES 81
Basic Dress. 81
Double Bodice 84
Bodice Overlay 100
Bodice Tucks and Trim. 98
Bow 87
Collar with Lace 92
Fake Bodice Tab. 103
Lace at Bottom Edge 92
Lace on Front Bodice. 93
Neckline Ruffles 95
Neckline Ruffle with Binding. 96
Stand-up Ruffle 95
Panties 107
Round Neck. 94
Skirt and Blouse Look 102
Skirt Tucks 100
Skirt with Ruffles 91
Tiered Skirt 89
Decorative Bands. 90

SECTION V   PAJAMAS & NIGHTGOWNS 109
Girl's Nightshirt 115
Pajamas. 109
Short Leg Pajama Bottoms
with Lace. 113
Snaps at Waist. 112

SECTION VI APPLIQUES, IDEAS & GIFTS 117
Appliques 117
Door Name 131
Handy Bag 128
Monograms 125
Sleeping Bag. 129
Toy Scoop. 126

LIST OF PATTERNS PIECES INCLUDED IN MASTER
PATTERN. 133

YARDAGE REQUIREMENTS 134

general sewing information

When you are sewing for toddlers, there are a couple of important points which you must bear in mind. Toddler's are active; they are crawling, walking and climbing; they need clothes which are not confining. They do not want anything tight pulled over their heads so, for example, if you are constructing a T-shirt for a one or two year old, we suggest using snaps on one shoulder as their heads are still very large compared to the other body measurements. For a three or four year old, make certain that the neck opening is large enough too so that the garment can easily be pulled over the head.

At this age, children become interested in trying to dress and undress themselves so their clothes should be easy to take off and put on. The following chart will give you some idea of what to expect from a toddler as far as dressing and undressing is concerned.

1 year
Extends one arm or leg to help you get them dressed.

1½ years
Can take off mittens and hats. Can unzip zippers and remove loose socks.

2 years
Can find large armholes and put their arms into them.

3 years
Starts to get interested in undressing, yet still needs help. Interested in dressing but does not know the front from the back. Can unbutton buttons.

4 years
Knows front from back. Can dress or undress without help.

When choosing the fabric for children's clothes, it is very important that you pick fabric which is colorfast as one garment that runs could ruin an entire wash. Before you cut out any garment, we recommend that you prewash the fabric as most fabric shrinks to a certain degree. The fabric should also withstand repeated washing as some children love to get dirty; playing in the sandbox or digging in the mud. How many times have you seen a child go out of his way to walk through a puddle? There are exceptions to this as some children like to stay clean and neat. Parents of these children are lucky as they do not know the frustration of changing a child's clothes only to have them dirty five minutes later.

Not only should the fabric have to withstand repeated washings, but it must be strong enough to take hard wear, especially at the knees.

The type of fabric depends upon the garment you are going to construct. For T-shirts, we recommend a single knit; it can be made from cotton, a blend of polyester and cotton, or in a colder climate you can use stretch terry or velour. For overalls, coveralls and pants, you can use either double knit fabric, heavy cotton fabric, denim, corduroy or permanent press. Try to find fabric which is wrinkle-resistant and does not need to be ironed.

Before you try on a garment on a child to see if it fits correctly, be careful to remove all pins. This is important; one pin prick may not hurt the child very much but it may be the last garment he or she will let you try on for a long time. If you are using a fabric with a nap like stretch terry, make certain that there are no pins hidden in the fabric.

The color of the fabric is not as important as it used to be. Usually you can use the same color fabric for either a boy or a girl. It used to be that boys wore dark and girls wore lighter colors. This is no longer true. Except for little girl's dresses, the clothes worn by toddlers are pretty much the same; T-shirts and shorts to T-shirts and slacks seem to be the everyday outfit for both girls and boys.

PATTERNS

Toddler's sizes vary from size 1 to 4. They have a diaper allowance. There is a MASTER PATTERN included with this book inside the back cover. This Master Pattern can be used for a wide variety of garments, such as T-shirts, sweaters, shirts, pants, shorts, overalls, coveralls, jumpsuits, dresses and panties. You can obtain a lot of variations of these garments by making some minor changes. These changes are explained in detail in the particular section where they apply. When you are constructing toddlers' garments, do not hesitate to use the same pattern for both boys and girls as the patterns are the same. The illustration in the book may have a boy's picture; this pattern can be used if you are planning to sew for a girl. This applies to all toddler patterns except girl's dresses and underpants.

The Master Patterns are designed for both stretch and non-stretch fabric. The Master Patterns are printed on both sides of the paper. We recommend that you trace the pattern so that you can use the Master Pattern over and over again for all types of garments.

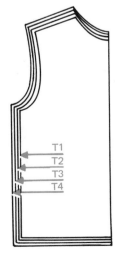

All the Master Patterns have a ¼" (6 mm) seam allowance included for all seams, unless otherwise specified on the pattern. This is the most common seam allowance used when sewing children's clothes. The Master Pattern has four sizes for each design, Sizes T1, T2, T3 and T4. Each size is color coded to make it easy for you to trace the pattern.

11

As children vary considerably in size, be sure to measure your child for width and length. Compare child's measurements to the chart below and choose the size closest to child's measurements. Make any adjustments necessary on the pattern.

BODY MEASUREMENTS — TODDLER

	T1	T2	T3	T4
Height	31″ (79 cm)	34″ (86 cm)	37″ (94 cm)	40″ (102 cm)
Chest	20″ (51 cm)	21″ (53.5 cm)	22″ (56 cm)	23″ (58.5 cm)
Waist	20″ (51 cm)	20½″ (52 cm)	21″ (53.5 cm)	21½″ (54.5 cm)
Hip	20½″ (52 cm)	21½″ (54.5 cm)	22½″ (57 cm)	23½″ (59.5 cm)

Diaper allowance is included in pattern.

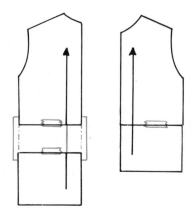

The most common adjustment which you have to make on a pattern is the length. You may want to either lengthen or shorten the pattern. Each Master Pattern has a line on the pattern indicating where to shorten or lengthen the pattern. Cut the pattern apart on that line, adjust the length by overlapping the pattern to shorten the garment, or tape a strip of paper between the two pieces equal to the amount you want to lengthen the pattern.

If any major adjustment has to be made on the pattern and you are not sure how to make the adjustment, refer to the book, "PROFESSIONAL PATTERN ALTERATIONS MADE EASY", published by KWIK-SEW Pattern Co., Inc.

If you would like to have additional designs for toddlers which are not included in the Master Pattern, you can obtain additional KWIK-SEW patterns for toddlers in your local fabric store. KWIK-SEW patterns are carried by most leading fabric stores in the United States, Canada and Australia. If your store does not have the patterns, they can obtain them for you.

KWIK-SEW patterns have at least three sizes included in each envelope and each size is marked in a different color, making it very easy for you to cut out the correct size. Complete easy-to-follow instructions are included with each pattern as well as instructions on how to properly set your sewing machine so that you can sew correctly on all types of fabric.

KWIK-SEW patterns are sized using the United States Government sizing specifications. To be certain that you are obtaining the correct size, check the sizes on the back of the pattern envelope and compare these with the actual body measurements. A certain amount of ease is included in the patterns. The amount of ease varies according to the design of the pattern, the style and type of the garment, and the type of fabric to be used. For example, a pattern for non-stretch fabric includes more ease than a pattern for stretch fabric.

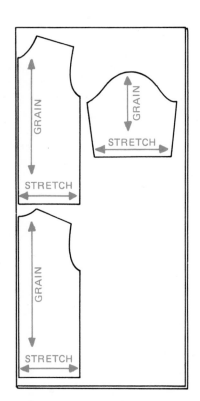

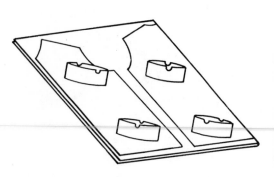

CUTTING

When cutting any type of fabric, it is very important to use a pair of sharp scissors so that you will obtain a clean cut. This is especially true if you are cutting stretch terry or a knitted fabric. Dull scissors have a tendency to chew the fabric rather than cut it. If they should become dull, get them sharpened as soon as possible. Never, we repeat, never use your sewing scissors for cutting anything else - especially paper! Cutting paper dulls the scissors very quickly.

When cutting out a garment using one-way stretch fabric, you have to be sure that the stretch goes around the body. If you do not do this, you will end up with a garment that is long and narrow after it has been used a few times. This is especially true when you use loosely knitted fabric. If you are using two-way stretch fabric, the fabric will always stretch more in one direction than the other. Again, the greatest degree of stretch goes around the body.

Regardless of the fabric you are using, always be sure to follow the arrows on the pattern pieces to be sure you have the grain and stretch of the fabric in the right direction in order to insure a proper fit.

Before cutting out the fabric, the usual procedure is to place the fabric right side to right side. However, sometimes it is necessary to cut some of the pattern pieces out of a single thickness of fabric. In this way you can often save on the amount of fabric you use. So, before you cut out any of the pieces, place all the pattern pieces on the fabric and figure out how to proceed.

All Master Patterns have a ¼" (6 mm) seam allowance. If you wish to change the seam allowance, this should be taken into consideration before you start cutting.

If you are working with fabric that stretches, try to keep the fabric on top of the table and not hanging down as this will tend to pull it out of shape and the pieces will not be identical with the pattern.

There is a possibility, when working with fine knits, that you will have runs if a dull pin cuts the thread in a loop. Because of this, it is very important that you use very fine pins with sharp points when you pin the pattern to the fabric. Some people prefer to use weights to hold the pattern pieces in place. Ash trays, cups, etc., will do very nicely as long as they keep the pattern steady on the fabric.

If you are using fabric that has a striped pattern, it is very important to line up the stripes before you start cutting.

If you are constructing a garment and you are using a fabric with a design or a color design either throughout the fabric or only on parts of the fabric, you have to be more careful when you cut out the garment so that the design matches at the seams. If the fabric has a design, measure the sleeve length first and cut out the sleeve.

Measure the distance from the design to the underarm point; line up the back and front pattern pieces so that the distance from the design to the underarm point is exactly the same; then cut out the back and the front pieces.

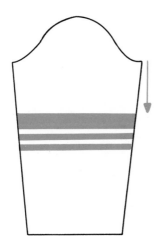

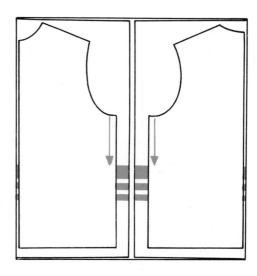

When you have cut out the pattern pieces, it is a good idea to mark each piece so that you do not mix them up. We recommend using transparent tape. This is the type of tape which you can sew through without the backing on the tape sticking to the needle. Place a small piece on the wrong side of the fabric marking the side seams, back, etc. This tape has a dull finish which you can write on. Always use a pencil, as a ballpoint pen could spot the garment and these spots are very difficult to wash out.

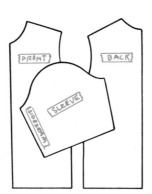

This tape can also be used for basting and has many other useful applications. As you read on you will find how this is done - plus you will discover many other shortcuts that rely on this tape. Be careful when you are using transparent tape on velour, stretch terry cloth, or other fabric with a similar surface, as it may mark the fabric. Try the tape on a piece of scrap fabric before you use it.

THREAD

The proper thread is very important when sewing. The basic rule to follow is to use cotton thread on cotton fabric and synthetic thread on synthetic fabric. As you will be washing the garments very often, it is important that you use a colorfast thread which will not shrink. Regardless of the type of thread you are using, always be sure to use the same thread on the top of the sewing machine as you use on the bobbin.

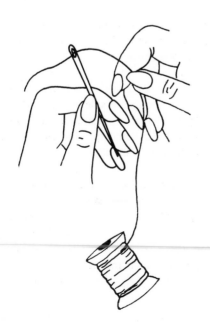

Almost all functions, when sewing toddler's clothes can be done on a sewing machine. However, in some cases you may have to sew a few stitches by hand, and the following should always be kept in mind if you are using synthetic thread. All synthetic thread is manufactured from synthetic fibers and these fibers tend to revert to their original shape. It is very important, when sewing by hand, that you always thread the needle from the end coming off the spool. If you do not follow this procedure, you will end up with small knots and fraying in the thread.

CORRECT TENSION

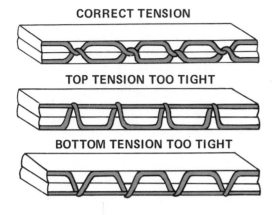

TOP TENSION TOO TIGHT

BOTTOM TENSION TOO TIGHT

SEWING

Before you start sewing, take a small piece of scrap fabric, double the fabric, and sew a straight stitch. Check the stitches to be sure the tensions are correct. The perfect thread tension results when the top and bottom tensions are exactly equal and the knot is buried in the fabric and cannot be seen. The best rule to follow is to adjust the tensions so that the stitch appears the same on both sides. See diagram. Try to adjust only the top tension as this is easier to do on all sewing machines, but in some cases you may have to adjust both the top and bottom tensions.

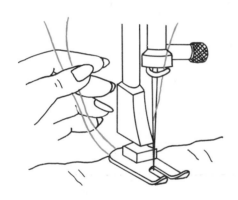

You will find it much easier to start a seam if you lower the needle into the fabric and hold both the top and bottom threads in your hand behind the presser foot. As the machine starts to sew, slowly pull these threads towards the rear of the machine. This will help the machine feed the material and eliminate the tendency of the material to bunch up under the presser foot.

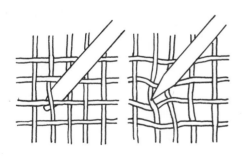

If your sewing machine has a tendency to skip stitches, this is usually caused by a dull or bent needle. The first thing you should do is to change the needle. We recommend using a fine needle No. 10 (70) or 12 (80) for knit fabric. Use No. 14 (90) for denim and corduroy.

If your machine continues to skip stitches and you are sewing on knit fabrics, we recommend that you use a ball point needle. This type of needle has a slightly rounded point, and, as a result, it tends to go between the fabric yarns rather than piercing the yarn and causing it to split or break.

It is also very important to use the correct pressure on the presser foot. Most of the up-to-date machines can be adjusted, which is usually simple to do. For woven and non-stretch fabric you should use normal pressure on the presser foot. For loosely knitted and very stretchy fabric you should loosen the pressure slightly on the presser foot.

When you are sewing terry cloth, stretch terry or any other fabric with a similar surface, it is sometimes difficult to sew the seam using the regular presser foot. The loops in the fabric get caught in the slot on the foot, and the fabric bunches up under the presser foot. A roller presser foot will eliminate this problem. The foot rolls over the fabric and you never have to worry that the fabric will bunch up under the roller presser foot.

SEAMS

The stitch you use should vary according to the type of fabric you are using and according to the size of the seam allowance. The type of sewing machine you are using will also be a factor in determining what kind of stitch you will use.

STRAIGHT STITCH MACHINE

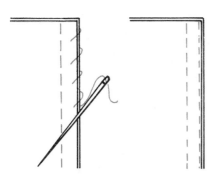

When you are using a ¼" (6 mm) seam allowance in non-stretch fabric, sew the seam using medium stitch length. Overcast the edges by hand if the fabric has a tendency to unravel, or stitch the seam allowance together close to the raw edges.

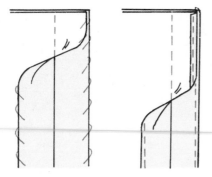

If you are using a 5/8" (1.5 cm) seam allowance, overcast the edges separately either by hand, or fold under the edge of the seam allowance and sew down the edges with a straight stitch.

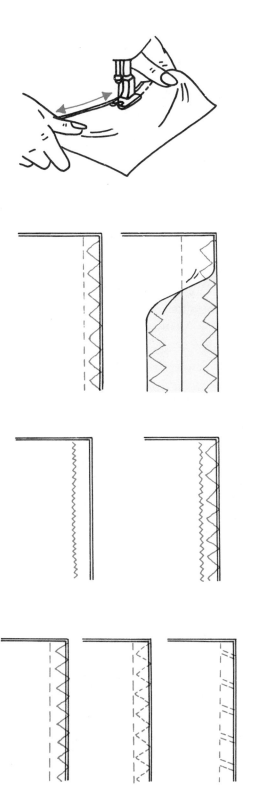

When sewing on stretch fabric, using any width seam allowance, stretch the fabric in back as well as in front of the presser foot as you sew the seams. We suggest that you sew the seam twice for greater strength. To prevent raveling, overcast the edges by hand.

ZIGZAG MACHINE

When you are using a ¼'' (6 mm) or a 5/8''(1.5 cm) seam allowance in non-stretch fabric, sew the seam using a medium length straight stitch. For a ¼'' (6 mm) seam allowance, overcast the raw edges together by using a zigzag stitch. For a 5/8'' (1.5 cm) seam allowance, overcast the edges separately.

For stretch fabric, sew the seam using a very narrow zigzag stitch. This will give you a strong seam with a certain degree of stretch. If the fabric has a tendency to unravel, overcast the edges with a large zigzag stitch.

REVERSE CYCLE MACHINE

When sewing on non-stretch fabric using ¼'' (6 mm) seam allowance, sew the seam with a medium length straight stitch, overcast the edges together with a zigzag stitch, or you can use a three-step zigzag stitch. On certain types of fabric you can use an overlock stitch to sew the seam and overcast in one operation. This saves you a great amount of time, as you do not have to sew the seam twice.

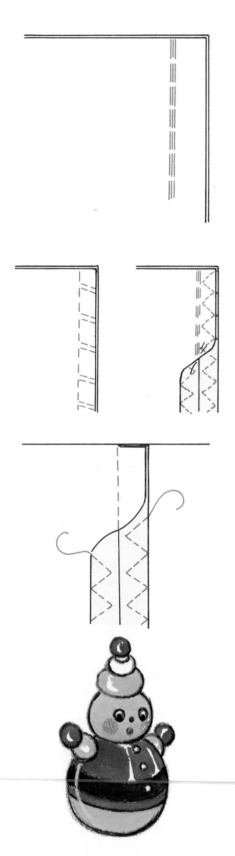

For a 5/8"(1.5 cm) seam allowance, sew the seams with a straight stitch except when you are sewing a seam on the bias or where there will be a lot of strain such as sewing in a sleeve or a crotch. Here we recommend that you use an elastic straight stitch. The machine sews two stitches forward and one stitch in reverse. This is a triple lock stitch which makes the seam strong and elastic.

When you are using a ¼" (6 mm) seam allowance on any type of stretch fabric, we recommend using an overlock stitch. This makes the seam both strong and elastic. For 5/8"(1.5 cm) seam allowance, sew the seam using an elastic straight stitch. Overcast the edges separately using a three-step zigzag.

To get a smooth, soft seam when you are sewing terry cloth, sew the seam with a straight stitch, open the seam allowance, and sew down the edges of the seam allowance with a three-step zigzag. This is a stitch where the machine sews three stitches on each zig and each zag. This stitch is almost invisible on the right side.

BIAS TAPE

A very easy way to finish the raw edges on many toddler's garments is to use bias tape. Bias tape is available in various sizes with either a single or double fold. The single fold tape is flat with folds on the outside and the raw edges together at the center of the tape. This type of tape should be folded once more, double, wrong side to wrong side to hide the raw edges. This is already done when you use double folded bias tape.

20

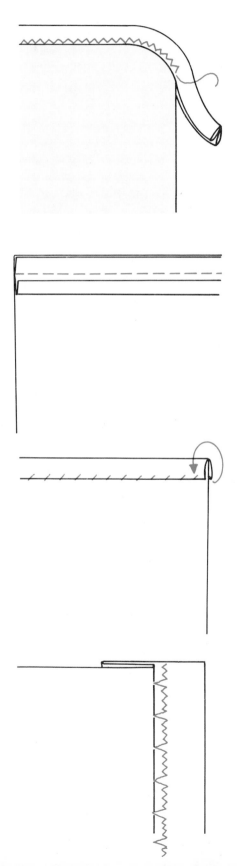

The easiest way to finish off raw edges of the fabric is to insert the raw edges of the fabric into the fold of the bias tape and sew close to the inner edge of the tape. Be sure to catch the tape on the wrong side. The easiest way to do this is to use a narrow zigzag stitch.

Another way to finish raw edges using bias tape is to unfold one side of the tape and place the right side of the tape on the wrong side of the garment with the raw edges of the tape matching the raw edges of the fabric. Sew a seam on the fold of the tape. Now fold the tape over the seam allowance to the right side. Topstitch from the right side close to the edge of the tape.

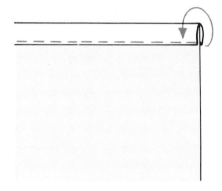

If you prefer not to have any seams showing on the right side, sew on the bias tape by placing the tape on the right side, raw edges together. Sew on the tape, fold the tape over the raw edges to the wrong side and stitch in place by hand.

HEMMING

The most common way to hem toddler's clothes is simply to fold the hem to the wrong side and sew down the hem with either a straight stitch, a small zigzag or a three-step zigzag stitch. If you want an invisible hem, for example, on a little girl's dress, do it either by hand or use a blind hem stitch. This stitch will be invisible on the right side.

PRESSING

It is very important to press the seams as you sew them; this is especially true for children's clothes which are small and it is extremely difficult to reach into the garment to press the seams after they have been finished.

It is also very important to use the correct type of iron and to set it at the temperature recommended for the fabric you are using. If you are not sure of the content of the fabric always use a cooler setting so that you are on the safe side. A hot iron used on polyester will melt the fabric; used on wool it could burn the material. This is so important that the American Wool Council suggests that you set your iron for "rayon" as the setting for "wool" is too hot on most irons.

A steam iron gives much better results when working with knit and stretch fabric. This is especially true when pressing sweater fabric. The steam does the work in shaping the garment.

The difference between ironing and pressing is that ironing is running the iron over the fabric in long back and forth strokes using pressure to remove creases and wrinkles in the fabric. Pressing is a press-lift, press-lift motion. You are applying both steam and heat to gently form the garment. When working with sweater fabric, the iron should actually not touch the fabric. The heat and steam do the work.

A pressing ham is very helpful, especially for form pressing the neckline on sweaters and T-shirts.

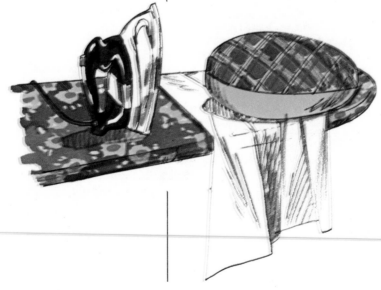

Before you cut out the fabric, be sure to press out the creases. Again, make sure that your iron is set for the correct temperature. Sometimes you will find fabric that has a crease which you cannot remove. In this case make sure, when you cut out the pattern, that this crease ends up in an inconspicuous place.

When you are making a seam using ¼'' (6 mm) seam allowance, first press the seam flat in the same grain direction as it was sewn. Then, press the seam allowance towards one side.

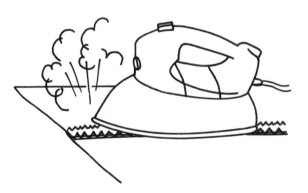

Even when using a larger seam allowance, always press the seam flat and then press the seam allowance open. Sometimes when you press open a seam the seam allowance will leave an imprint which shows on the right side. To eliminate this imprint, place a strip of paper under the seam allowance before you press it. Or, after you have pressed the seam, gently press under the edge of the seam allowance.

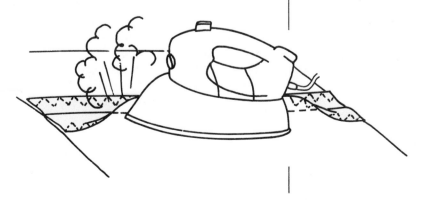

BUTTONS AND BUTTONHOLES

Before making a buttonhole, check the instruction book for your sewing machine as the procedure is different for different sewing machines. When you mark your buttonholes, we suggest that you make the buttonhole 1/8'' (2 mm) larger than the button. You can use either horizontal or vertical buttonholes for a blouse or shirt. If you are making vertical buttonholes, you make the buttonhole on the center front or center back line. If you are making horizontal buttonholes, start the buttonhole 1/8'' (2 mm) from the center front or center back line towards the edge of garment. Sew on the buttons on the center front or back line of the other piece. By following this procedure, the buttons will always end up at the center front or back.

Buttons can be sewn on either by machine or by hand. If you are using a machine, drop your feed dogs; set the machine for zigzag. The width of the stitch should be the same as the distance between the holes in the buttons. Again, refer to your sewing machine instruction book.

SNAPS

You will find it much easier in many instances to change a child's clothes if they have snaps instead of buttons and buttonholes. The easiest way to put on the snaps is by using a plier kit for snaps. This will save you a lot of time and make it much easier to attach the snaps. Make sure that you apply the snaps at the correct position, as it is almost impossible to change them. Remember that girl's clothing closes from the right and the boy's from the left. When you are using snaps, be very careful that all of the points of the prongs are enclosed in the ring. These points are very sharp, and if one is sticking out, it could scratch the child.

t-shirts, shirts, sweaters and blouses

T-shirts are probably the most practical garment in a toddler's wardrobe. Teamed with jumpsuits, shorts or slacks, they complete an outfit. They can be adapted to any season of the year by using long or short sleeves. Fortunately, a T-shirt is one of the simplest garments to make. You can use a wide variety of colors and fabric designs. Numerous attractive ensembles can be created by using different or contrasting colors for the sleeve and neckband or on a long sleeve shirt for the cuff and neckband. T-shirts may be very attractively personalized with the use of appliques or initials. How to do this is described in Section VI.

For the sleeves and neckband, we recommend using ribbing. For the T-shirt itself, single knit is the best fabric to use, since it is usually of lighter weight than double knit. Single or double knit is the method used to knit the fabric. The easiest way to tell the difference is to look at both sides of the fabric. Single knit looks smooth and finished on the right side only, while double knit looks almost the same on both sides in addition to being heavier.

Some people believe that single knit fabrics are always smooth and do not have any texture. This is no longer true. Machines have now been developed which give us beautiful finishes in a wide variety of textures.

Single knit usually comes in a double width, approximately 60'' (152 cm) wide. Because this fabric tends to roll at the edges, it is doubled and the edges knitted or sewn together at the mill. This makes it easier for the manufacturer or fabric stores to handle the rolls or bolts. Some single knit is knitted in a tubular shape. It is often difficult to see where edges are joined. In some instances, it looks like a flaw. This is where you should cut the material apart before proceeding. This will eliminate the possibility of ending up with this seam or flaw in the front or back, etc., where it will be very noticeable.

If you are not certain of the content, or, if you do not know the shrinkage factor, always be on the safe side by pre-shrinking in hot water before proceeding. Cotton should always be pre-shrunk if the label does not indicate that it has been shrunk at the mill.

You should also be careful, when cutting out the garment, that the crease in the fabric is not in a conspicuous place as this crease is very often difficult to press out.

T-SHIRT

The Master Pattern at the back of this book has a pattern for T-shirts with set-in sleeves. Trace off the Master Pattern 4-front, 5-back, trace cutting line A for the neckline.

Use Pattern 3 for the sleeves. Decide if you want short or long sleeves. If you plan to hem the sleeves or use cuffs or bands, be sure to follow the correct cutting line.

For the neckband and the armbands or cuffs, we recommend that you use ribbing which has to be cut across the grain so that most of the stretch goes lengthwise. For the neckband, use Pattern Piece No. 6. If you plan to have cuffs, use Pattern Piece No. 11 or you can purchase ready made cuffs. If you plan to have short sleeves, cut out Pattern Piece No. 30 for the armbands.

Fold the fabric double with the right sides together. Place the pattern pieces on the fabric. Be sure to always follow the arrows on the pattern pieces, as it is very important that the greatest degree of stretch goes around the body and around the arms. Cut out the front, the back and the sleeves.

Cut out the neckband and the armband from ribbing.

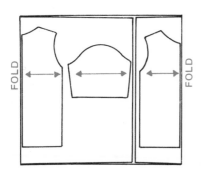

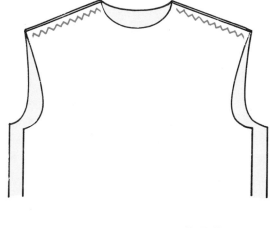

Start constructing a T-shirt with set-in sleeves by placing the back and the front, right side to right side, and sew the shoulder seams.

As a child's head is large compared to the rest of the body, be sure that the neck opening is large enough so that the garment easily slips over the head. If you prefer to have snaps on one shoulder so that it is easier to slip the garment over the head, this procedure is explained later in this section.

Sew the ends of the neckband together to form a circle, right side to right side. Fold and press the band double lengthwise, the wrong sides together.

Divide the neckband and the neck opening in fourths with pins.

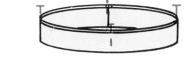

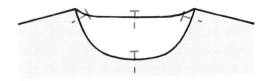

Pin the band to the neck opening on the right side, raw edges together, matching the pins.

Place the seam on the neckband on the center of the back. Children prefer the seam in the back so when they dress themselves they will know the front from the back of the garment. When sewing the neckband to the shirt, stretch the neckband between the pins so that it will fit the neck opening. The easiest way to do this is to always have the smallest piece on top. In this case, the neck opening is underneath and the neckband on top. When using stretch fabric, you always stretch the smaller piece to fit the larger. This is the opposite method used for sewing non-stretch fabric, where you always ease the larger piece to the smaller.

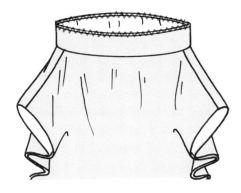

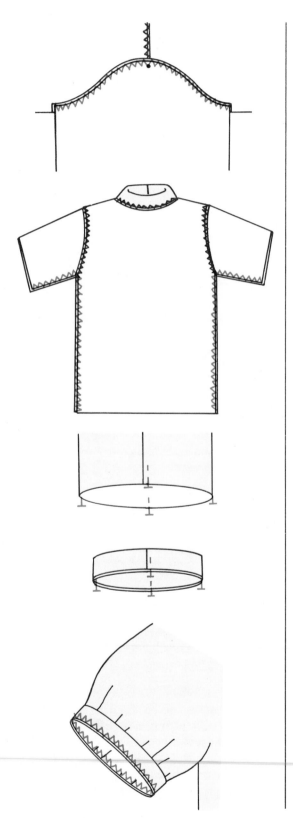

Sew in the sleeves by matching the underarm edges and the dot on the cap of the sleeve to the shoulder seam.

Sew the side seam and sleeve seam in one continuous operation, starting at the bottom of the shirt.

Use the same procedure to finish either a long or a short sleeve. Sew the ends of the sleeve bands together, right side to right side to form circles. Fold each band lengthwise, wrong sides together. Divide the bands and the sleeve openings in half with pins.

Pin the bands to the right side of the sleeve openings, matching the pins and the raw edges. Sew on the bands, stretching the bands to fit the openings.

It is not necessary to have an armband or cuff on the sleeves. Instead just fold the fabric to the wrong side and hem either by machine or by hand. Hem the bottom edge of the T-shirt.

RIBBING NECKBAND WITH RUFFLED EDGE

A pretty variation for a little girl's T-shirt can be made by using a wider neckband finished with a lettuce edging. Cut the neckband 8'' (20 cm) wide and the same length as the pattern piece. Sew the neckband to the neck opening as previously described. To obtain the ruffled effect on the neckband, set your sewing machine at a wide zigzag width and a short stitch length. Using a zigzag stitch, sew the outer edge of the neckband, stretching the edge as much as possible while sewing. Fold over the neckband to the right side.

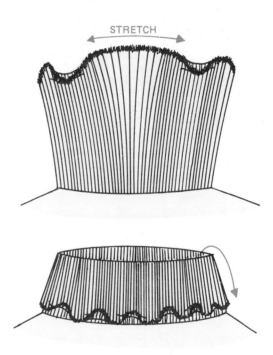

To obtain this same effect on a long sleeve T-shirt, use Pattern Piece No. 11 for the cuff and follow the same procedure as used for the neckband.

SNAPS AT ONE SHOULDER

It is a very simple matter to change the pattern so that you have snaps on one shoulder. On the back and front pattern piece, extend the length 1¼'' (3.2 cm) on the left shoulder (see illustration). Use the same pattern for the neckband and add 1'' (2.5 cm) to the length of the band for the overlap.

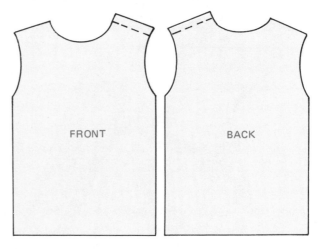

Sew the shoulder seam which is not extended. To stabilize the fabric under the snaps, cut two pieces of woven fabric or lightweight interfacing 1'' (2.5 cm) wide and the length of the shoulder. Place on the wrong side of the shoulder on the front and the back and overcast the raw edges together.

Fold the neckband double lengthwise, right sides together, and sew across the short ends. Turn the band right side out.

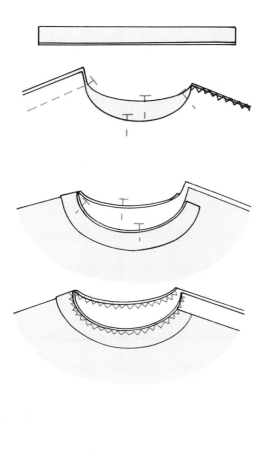

Divide the neckline and the neckband in fourths with pins. Divide the neckline from folding line on the front and the back 1'' (2.5 cm) from the edge of the front and back shoulder.

Pin the neckband to the neckline, right sides and raw edges together, matching the pins, and placing the finished ends of the band on the folding lines of the front and back shoulder.

Fold the front and back shoulder facing on the folding line over the band to the right side. Sew on the band, including the facing in the seam. Stretch the band while sewing to fit the opening. Turn the facings to the wrong side.

Attach the shoulder facing to the shirt by topstitching, using a three-step zigzag or a small zigzag stitch.

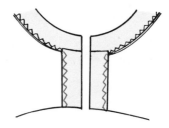

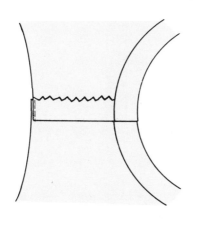

Overlap the front shoulder over the back shoulder 1'' (2.5 cm). To keep the shoulder in place, sew a seam across, close to the sleeve opening.

Finish the rest of the shirt as previously described.

Attach two snaps at the shoulder. If you prefer, you may use buttons and buttonholes instead of snaps.

FAKE OPENING

A variation for a regular T-shirt is to make a fake opening by cutting a strip of firm ribbing or a contrasting fabric 2½" (6.5 cm) wide and 7" (18 cm) long. Fold the strip double lengthwise. Sew a seam on the long side. Move this seam so that it is in the middle of the strip, sew across one short side. Turn the strip right side out.

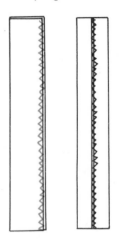

Place this band at the center front of the T-shirt with the unsewn edge even with the neckline and sew across. Sew on the neckband as previously described.

Attach the band to the front of the T-shirt by sewing on three buttons through the band and the shirt.

RUGBY SHIRT

Most Rugby shirts have a contrasting collar and facing. However, this is not really necessary. These shirts were originally worn in England and the colors of the shirts determined the different Rugby teams.

For the Rugby shirt, use Pattern Piece 4-front, 5-back, use cutting line B at the neck opening, 3-sleeve, 9-collar, 7-front facing.

A Rugby shirt can be made with a short sleeve; in this case simply hem the sleeve. For a long sleeve, you can use a cuff as described for T-shirts. If you wish to use regular Rugby shirt cuffs, use Pattern Piece No. 12.

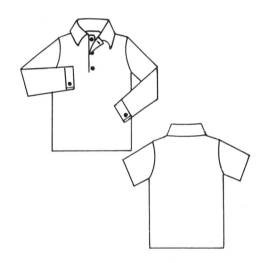

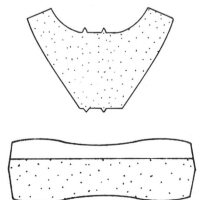

Cut out the pattern pieces.

You can construct the Rugby shirt with or without interfacing for the collar, front facing and cuffs. If you plan to use interfacing, use lightweight press-on interfacing; press on the interfacing on the wrong side of the fabric.

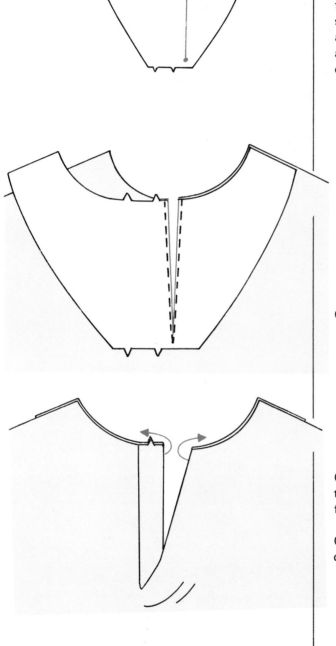

When you have cut out all the pattern pieces, mark a line for the front slit on the wrong side of the facing piece. Pin the facing to the front, right sides together. <u>On the left</u> side of the neckline, <u>the raw edges should be together</u>. Sew a straight seam 1/8″ (3 mm) on one side of the line starting at the neckline, pivot at the end of the slit and sew the other seam also 1/8″ (3 mm) from the marked line.

Cut an opening in between the lines to the bottom of the slit.

On the right front, fold the tab facing on the folding line to the inside and press. This will form the tab. Fold the facing on the left front to the inside.

Overlap the left front over the right front, matching the center front and pin to keep it in place.

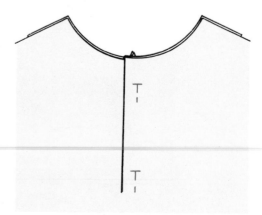

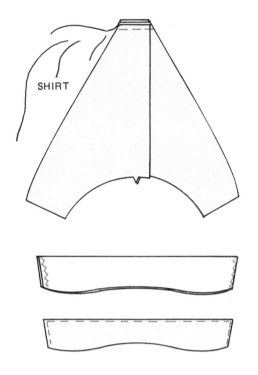

SHIRT

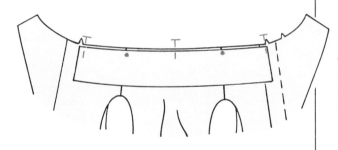

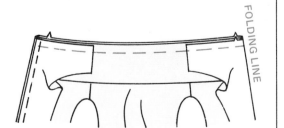

FOLDING LINE

From the inside, stitch across the bottom edge of the facing and tab through all thicknesses.

Place the back and the front, right side to right side, and sew the shoulder seams.

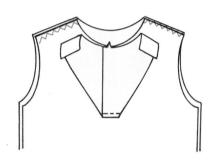

Fold the collar double lengthwise, right sides together, and stitch the ends. Trim the corners. Turn the collar right side out and press.

Pin the collar to the right side of the neckline, matching the center back, dots to the shoulder seams and the ends of the collar to the center front. Bear in mind that on the right side, the center front is in the middle of the tab. On the left side, the center front is on the shirt part.

On the right front, fold the facing on folding line to the right side over the collar, matching the notches for the center front. The facing will extend ¼'' (6 mm) beyond the shoulder seam. Pin through all layers.

On the left front, fold the facing to the right side over the collar. Pin the facing to the neckline through all layers; facing extends ¼'' (6 mm) past the shoulder seam. Sew on the collar to the neckline through all layers.

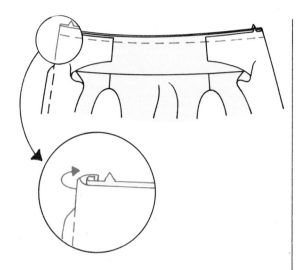

If desired, facing may be sewn to the left front so the edge of the facing will show from the outside resembling piping. If this effect is desired, pin the seam allowance of the slit toward the shirt. Fold the facing 1/8'' (3 mm) from the seam on the facing side. The 1/8'' (3 mm) will form a lip on the right side and it will resemble piping. Stitch the collar to the facing through all layers.

Turn facing to the inside. Understitch the seam allowance to the back at the back neckline. Attach the ends of the facing to the shoulder seams.

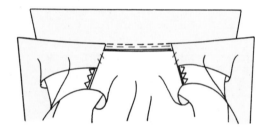

Sew the sleeves in place by matching the center top of the sleeve with the shoulder seam and the sleeve seam to the side seam.

Sew the side seam and the sleeve seam in one continuous operation, starting at the bottom of the shirt.

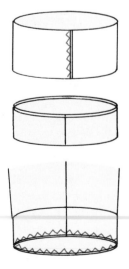

CUFF WITH BUTTONS AND BUTTONHOLES

Use Master Pattern number 12 for the cuffs. Stitch the ends of each cuff, right sides together, to form circles. Fold each cuff double lengthwise, wrong sides together.

Pin the cuff to the bottom edge of the sleeve, right sides and raw edges together, matching the cuff seam to the sleeve seam. Sew on the cuff.

Fold the cuff in half on the seam line. On the fold, opposite the seam, make a vertical buttonhole, through all thicknesses, ½" (1.3 cm) from the fold. Sew on a button on each back half of the cuff, approximately 1" (2.5 cm) from the buttonhole.

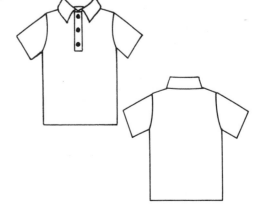

Make vertical buttonholes on the left front. Sew on the buttons to match the buttonholes. If desired, snaps can be used instead of buttons and buttonholes.

Hem the bottom of the shirt.

FRONT TAB SHIRT

Another attractive variation for a toddler's shirt is to use a front tab. You can also dress up the front with small pockets. Use Master Pattern No. 27 or 29 for the pockets. These pockets may be used on any other type shirt. For the front tab shirt, use Master Pattern Pieces: 4-front, 5-back, follow Cutting Line B for the neck opening and follow cutting line for tab at center front. For the sleeve, use Pattern Piece 3, collar-9, tab-8. Decide if you prefer to have short or long sleeves. The sleeves can be finished using any of the methods described for T-shirts and Rugby shirts. You can use press-on interfacing for the collar and the tab.

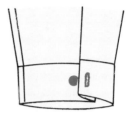

This type of shirt can be constructed from a solid color fabric, striped, checked or any other design. When you are using other than a solid color fabric, it is very important to match the design on the bottom of both the front and the back pattern pieces. The sleeves are matched underneath the arm. It is also very important to match the tab in the front to the front of the shirt.

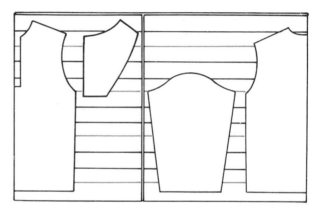

For this shirt, you should use a knit fabric for the body and the sleeves. The tab facing and collar can be made from woven fabric. You can use the same fabric as you used for a pair of pants and you will have a matching outfit. Just be sure that the fabric is not too heavy.

If you are using a vertical stripe or check, line up the center front of the tab along the same stripe or check as you used on the center front of the shirt. If you do not wish to match the tab with the shirt front, you can cut the tab in the opposite direction. Or, as a variation, you may use a solid contrasting color.

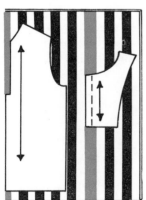

Cut out the pattern pieces. At the center front, cut the front opening following the line on the pattern.

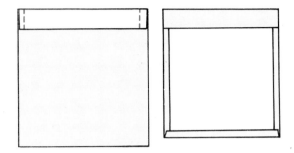

If you are going to have pockets, we suggest that you sew on the pockets before you start the actual construction of the shirt. Fold the top of the pocket on the folding line to the right side. Sew each side of overlap using ¼'' (6 mm) seam allowance.

Turn to the wrong side. It is much easier to sew on the pocket if you press it first. Fold the pocket edges under ¼'' (6 mm) to the wrong side and press.

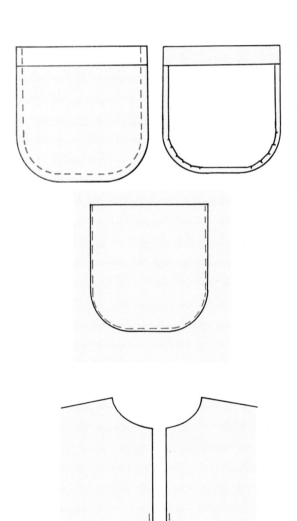

If the pocket has a round bottom, it is easier to press the edge if you sew around the bottom of the pocket ¼'' (6 mm) in from the edge and then press the seam allowance to the wrong side following the stitching line.

Pin the pocket in place and topstitch around the sides and bottom close to the edge.

On the bottom of the front opening, staystitch across the bottom and up 1'' (2.5 cm) on each side on the seam line. Press each tab facing on the folding line, wrong sides together. Unfold the tabs.

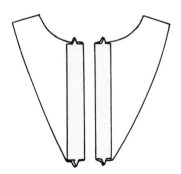

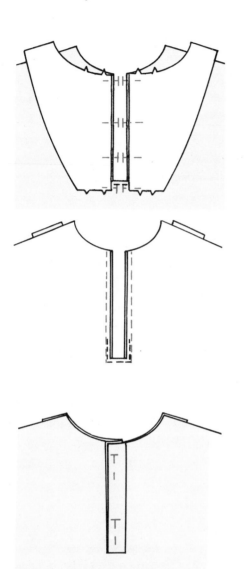

Place the tabs on each side of the front opening, right side to right side, raw edges together and pin. The tab will extend ½" (1.3 cm) below the opening.

Begin sewing the seam at the neck opening using ¼" (6 mm) seam allowance. Stop sewing ¼" (6 mm) from the end of the tab (bottom of staystitching). Clip the seam allowance on the front to the corner of the staystitching.

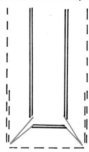

Turn the tab facing to the wrong side on the folding line. Pin in place.

For a boy, overlap the left tab over the right tab, matching the notches at the neckline and the bottom edges. For a girl, overlap the right tab over the left tab. Pin together.

On the wrong side, secure the ends of the tabs to the front by sewing across the bottom edge of the tabs between the seams, following the staystitching line. If you would like to reinforce the bottom of the tab, sew a rectangle on the edge to keep the tab facing in place.

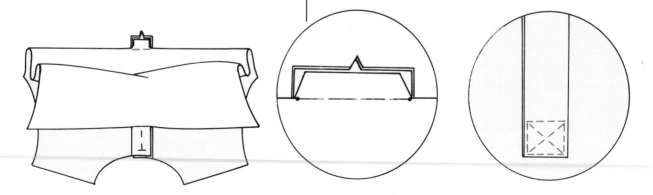

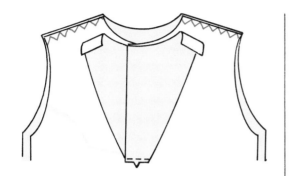

Place the back and the front, right side to right side, and sew the shoulder seams.

Fold the collar on the folding line, right sides together. Sew the ends. Trim the corners. Turn right side out and press. If you would like to have a round collar for a girl, use Master Pattern No. 10.

Place collar pieces right side together, and sew around the collar, leaving the neckline open. Clip seam allowance. Turn collar right side out and press.

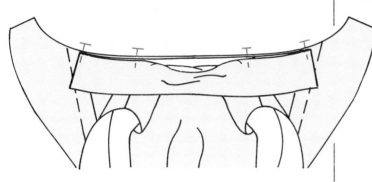

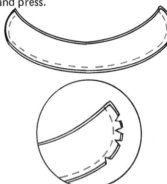

If you wish, you can topstitch the collar ¼'' (6 mm) from the edge.

Pin the collar to the right side of the neck opening, matching the center back and the dots on the collar to the shoulder seams and the ends of the collar at the center front. Pin only the undercollar to the back neckline.

Fold the facing on the folding line to the right side over the collar. Clip the seam allowance on the upper collar at the end of the facing.

Sew on the collar by sewing through all layers the width of the facing. Continue sewing only the under collar to the back neck opening and through all the layers the width of the facing on the other side. Turn the facing to the wrong side.

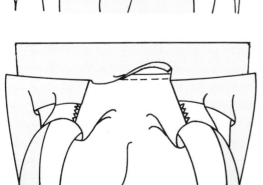

Clip the seam allowance at the end of the facing. Press the seam allowance of the back neckline towards the collar. Fold under the seam allowance of the upper collar and pin over the neckline seam to cover the stitches.

41

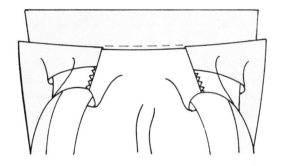

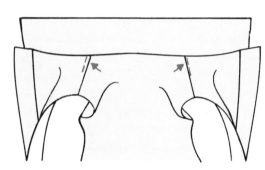

Stitch close to the folded edge of the upper collar through all layers. Attach the ends of the facing to the shoulder seams by hand, or machine.

An easy way to attach the facings to the shoulder seam is to stitch from the right side of the garment as close as possible to the shoulder seam, stitching through the shirt and facing.

Sew the sleeves and side seams. Hem the bottom of the shirt and finish the ends of the sleeves in the same manner as previously described.

Make vertical buttonholes on the center of the left front of the tab for a boy, on right front for a girl. Now, sew on the buttons to match the buttonholes in the center of the other tab. If the collar is to be worn open, the top button and buttonhole can be eliminated.

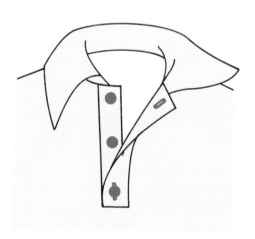

FULL FRONT OPENING

For a full front opening, use the following Master Pattern pieces. Back-5, front-4; cut the pattern using Cutting Line B for the neck opening.

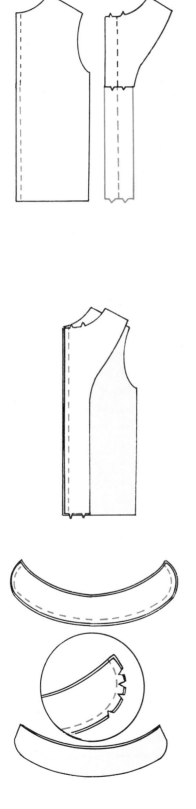

At the center front, cut the front opening following the line on the pattern. Extend this cut all the way down to the bottom of the front. Use Pattern Piece No. 3 for the sleeves and No. 9 or 10 for the collar. For the front tab, use Pattern Piece No. 8. It is necessary to extend the length of the tab facing the same length as the front. Decide if you want long or short sleeves and how you want to finish the ends of the sleeves. Cut out the pattern pieces.

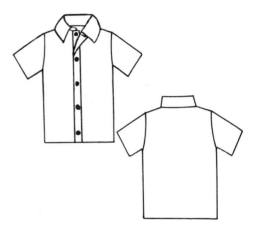

Fold the tab facing on the folding line, wrong sides together, and press. Unfold the tab facing. Place the front tab facing on the front edge of the shirt with the right sides together and sew from the neckline to the bottom edge of the shirt. Press the seam allowance toward the tab.

Sew the front to the back at the shoulder seams.

If you are using the rounded collar, place the collar pieces, right sides together, and sew around the collar, leaving the neckline open. Clip the seam allowance. Turn the collar right side out and press.

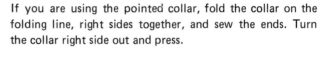

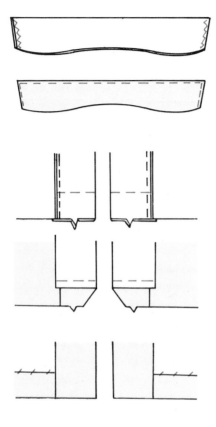

If you are using the pointed collar, fold the collar on the folding line, right sides together, and sew the ends. Turn the collar right side out and press.

Sew the rest of the shirt as previously described.

Finish the bottom edge of the front facing by folding the facing on the folding line to the right side. Sew across the width of the facing at the desired hemline. Trim the hem on the facing. Turn the facing to the inside of the garment. Hem the bottom edge of the shirt.

On the inside, pin the facing over the seam allowance with the facing extending ¼" (6 mm) past the seam.

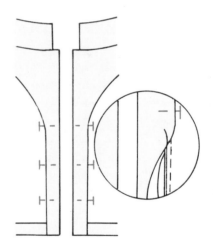

On the right side of the shirt, topstitch on each tab ¼" (6 mm) from the edges of the tab.

Make the buttonholes on the right front for a girl and on the left front for a boy. Make vertical buttonholes in the middle of the tab. Sew on the buttons to match the buttonholes.

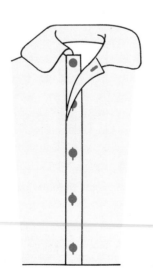

SWEATERS

Many people are amazed when they find out that it is possible to construct a beautiful sweater on a sewing machine. The first question they ask is, "Will the fabric unravel when you cut it?" The answer is "No." This is the same method as used by sweater manufacturers. Because of the way the fabric is knitted, the loops tend to lock into each other when the fabric is cut.

Sweaters are one of the fastest and easiest garments which you can make, and you should be able to complete it in less than thirty minutes. The reason for this is that most sweater fabric has a finished ribbing which is used for the bottom of the sweater and the sleeves. This eliminates all hemming.

Sweater fabric is available in a large variety of fibers, designs, texture and weights.

There are three basic types of sweater fabric; sweater bodies, sweater blankets and sweater yardage. The yarn can be the same for all three types. The difference is determined by the type of knitting machine on which the fabric was made.

A sweater body, also known as a sweater tube, is circular in shape. There is a "run" which looks like a flaw the length of the sweater tube. This is not a flaw and it is where you should cut the fabric open before you proceed to cut out the garment. If you do not do this, the flaw might appear in the sweater.

A sweater blanket comes already cut open. One edge of both the sweater body and the blanket is finished with ribbing. This ribbing is for the bottom of the sweater and the bottom of the sleeves.

You can also find sweater fabric in the form of yardage. When you use sweater yardage, you must hem the sleeves and the bottom of the sweater or you can use self-fabric. You may sew on special cuffs, or finish the bottom with a special trim. Stores which carry sweater fabric usually carry ribbing, which is used around the neck opening. This ribbing may also be used for the cuffs. If you are unable to obtain ribbing, you can use the sweater fabric, if you cut it across the grain.

When you choose a sweater fabric for a toddler, there are two important considerations which you should keep in mind. The fabric must be easy to care for and it should not be rough or scratchy. Try not to pick a fabric that has to be dry cleaned. Synthetic fabric is the best and the best synthetic is Orlon. It is both soft and easy to care for. When you wash an Orlon sweater, we suggest that you turn it inside out as it has a tendency to pill.

When you are constructing a pullover sweater, you use the same pattern pieces and techniques as you use for a T-shirt. Regardless of the weight of the fabric, variety, etc., the sewing technique is the same.

Before you cut out the fabric, check the measurements with the pattern, so that you are sure you obtain the correct length for the body and the sleeves.

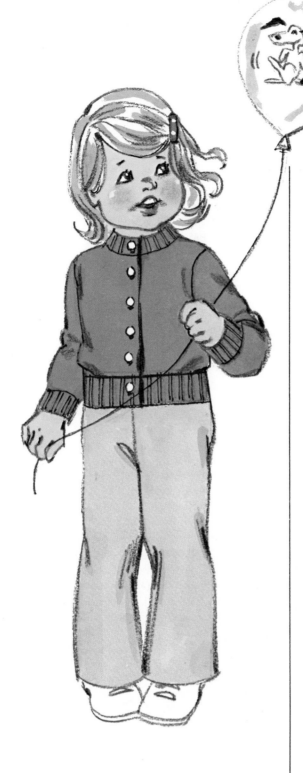

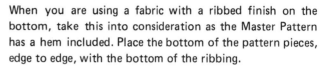

When you are using a fabric with a ribbed finish on the bottom, take this into consideration as the Master Pattern has a hem included. Place the bottom of the pattern pieces, edge to edge, with the bottom of the ribbing.

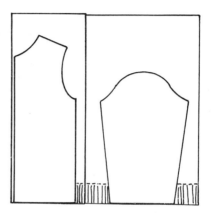

If you would like to have a cardigan style with buttons in the front, add ¾'' (2 cm) to the pattern at the center front and cut the front open.

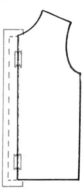

For the neckband, cut a straight piece of fabric or ribbing across the grain 2'' (5 cm) wide and 9'' (23 cm) long. You can make the neckband wider if you desire. As the stretch factor varies in different types of ribbing or fabric, be sure to cut a long enough strip. To get the correct size for the neckband, stretch the band around the neck so that it feels comfortable. Add 1'' (2.5 cm) for the overlap. Cut off the excess fabric. Fold and press the neckband double lengthwise with the wrong sides together.

Sew the shoulder seams.

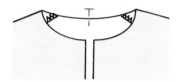

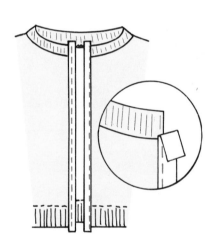

Divide the band in half. Pin the band to the right side of the neck opening with the raw edges together. Match the center back of the sweater with the center of the band. The ends of the band should end up at the edge of the front. Sew on the band. Stretch the band as you sew to fit the neck opening.

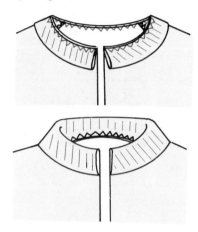

The easiest method of finishing the front of a cardigan is with a strip of grosgrain ribbon. We recommend that you preshrink the ribbon before you use it. Cut two lengths of ½" (1.3 cm) wide grosgrain ribbon long enough for the front plus 1" (2.5 cm). Overlap the ribbon on the right side of each front, ¼" (6 mm); ½" (1.3 cm) should extend up from the neckband and the bottom edge. Sew on the ribbon close to the inner edge with a straight stitch.

Fold under the bottom and the top of the ribbon. Turn the ribbon to the wrong side and secure the ribbon to the neckline and the bottom edge with a few stitches by hand. The buttonholes and buttons will keep the ribbon in place.

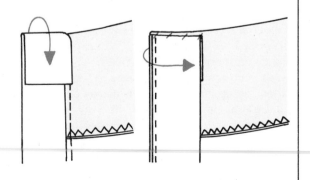

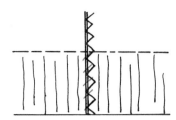

Sew on the sleeves as previously described. Sew the sleeve seams and the side seams in one continuous operation. Attach the seam allowance to one side at the bottom edge of the sleeves and the side seams if you are using a sweater body with a finished bottom edge.

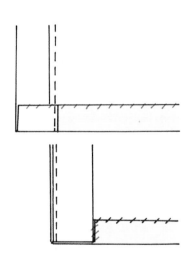

If you are making a sweater without a finished bottom edge, turn the hem to the wrong side and hem. Then fold the ribbon to the wrong side and attach it to the bottom edge of the hem with a few stitches by hand.

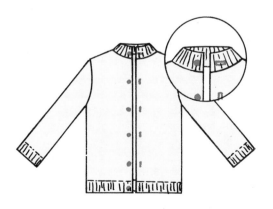

BUTTONS AND BUTTONHOLES

On a round neck cardigan, the top buttonhole is horizontal on the neckband and other buttonholes are vertical. The buttonholes should be placed in the middle of the grosgrain ribbon.

For a boy's cardigan, place the buttonholes on the left front; for a girl's, on the right front.

It is difficult to make buttonholes by hand when sewing on sweater fabric. It can be done, but you must be very careful; for, if you do not sew the stitches very close together, you may get a run in the sweater fabric.

49

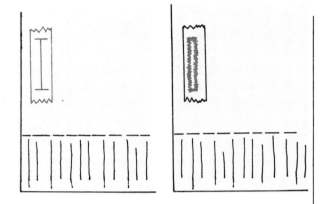

It is much easier to make buttonholes using a sewing machine, and there is much less chance of getting a run. As sweater fabric is very soft and sometimes has large loops, it is difficult for the machine to feed the material, and the loops often catch in the presser foot. To overcome this, place a strip of transparent tape where you are going to sew the buttonhole. Use the type of tape you can write on. Mark the position and size of the buttonhole with a pencil. Use slightly longer stitches than when sewing regular fabric. Sew the buttonhole through the tape; remove the tape when the buttonhole is completed.

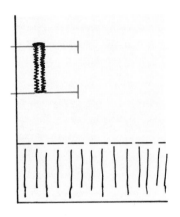

When you cut open the buttonholes, it is a good idea to place a pin at the end of the buttonhole at cross angles to the buttonhole. This will prevent you from cutting too large a hole, and perhaps ruining the garment.

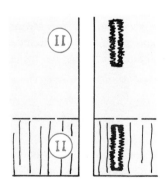

After you remove the tape, you may find that there are small pieces which are difficult to remove. You can remove these pieces by using a steam iron. Do not touch the garment with the iron. The heat from the steam will cause the small pieces of tape to curl up, and they can then be brushed off.

Buttons can be sewn on either by hand or by machine. If you are using a sewing machine, we suggest that you place transparent tape where you are going to sew on the buttons. The tape prevents the soft fabric from pulling up into the holes in the buttons. Mark the position of the buttons. It should be 1/8" (3 mm) down from the top of the buttonhole. Drop the feed dogs; set the machine for zigzag. The width of the stitch should be the same as the distance between the holes in the buttons. Refer to your sewing machine instruction book.

jumpsuits, coveralls, overalls, slacks and shorts

All the patterns in the first part of this section are for knit and stretch fabric only. The type of fabric you use will depend upon which garment you are constructing but it has to be a stretch fabric.

Jumpsuits are a very practical as well as attractive garments. They are excellent for both playing and for dress-up occasions. You can make the jumpsuit in one solid color or you can have the body in one color and the sleeves and collar in a different color. It can be made with no pockets or with many pockets. The jumpsuit can be of one solid color with the sleeves and patches on the knees in a contrasting color.

Trace off the Master Pattern for the jumpsuit; 1-front, 2-back, 3-sleeves, follow cutting line A for the neckline. For the collar, you can use either Pattern Piece No. 9 or No. 10. No. 9 is a pointed collar; No. 10 is a round collar.

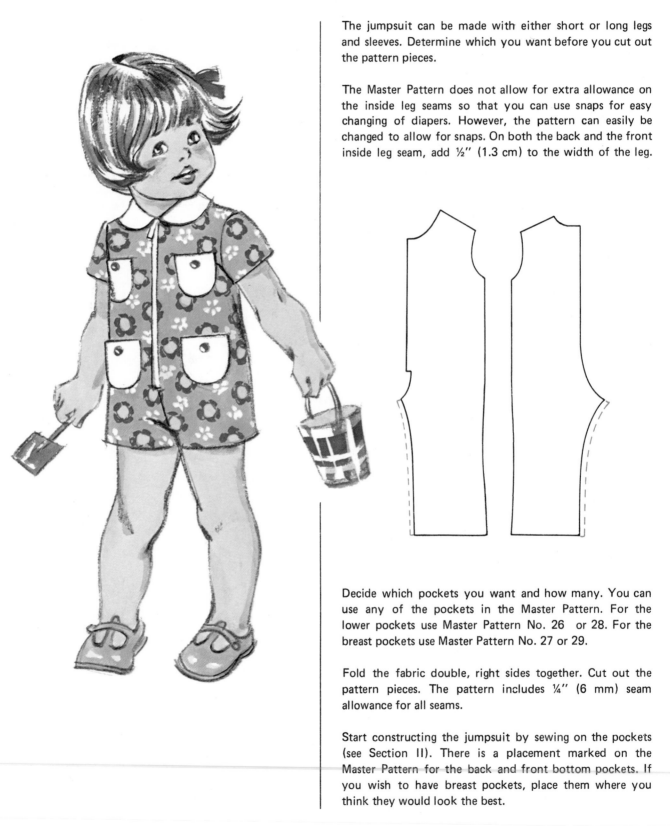

The jumpsuit can be made with either short or long legs and sleeves. Determine which you want before you cut out the pattern pieces.

The Master Pattern does not allow for extra allowance on the inside leg seams so that you can use snaps for easy changing of diapers. However, the pattern can easily be changed to allow for snaps. On both the back and the front inside leg seam, add ½" (1.3 cm) to the width of the leg.

Decide which pockets you want and how many. You can use any of the pockets in the Master Pattern. For the lower pockets use Master Pattern No. 26 or 28. For the breast pockets use Master Pattern No. 27 or 29.

Fold the fabric double, right sides together. Cut out the pattern pieces. The pattern includes ¼" (6 mm) seam allowance for all seams.

Start constructing the jumpsuit by sewing on the pockets (see Section II). There is a placement marked on the Master Pattern for the back and front bottom pockets. If you wish to have breast pockets, place them where you think they would look the best.

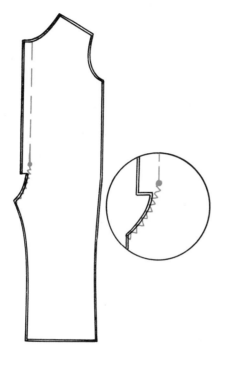

Sew the front crotch seam from the inside leg seam to the dot at the end of the zipper opening, lock the stitches and baste from the dot to the neckline using a 5/8'' (1.5 cm) seam allowance. Press the center front seam open.

Place a closed zipper face down on the opened seam allowances, placing the middle of the zipper teeth along the basted seam. Place the zipper pull ½'' (1.3 cm) down from the neckline. Baste the zipper to the SEAM ALLOWANCE ONLY. An easy way to keep the zipper in place is to tape across the zipper using transparent tape; this would eliminate the basting.

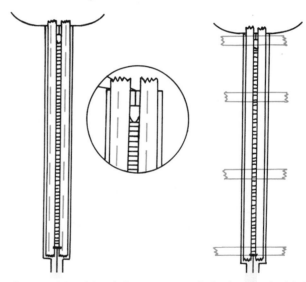

On the right side of the garment, stitch along each side ¼'' (6 mm) from the center front seam and across the bottom edge of zipper. Remove the center front basting or tape, if used.

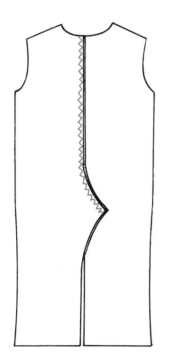

Sew the center back seam.

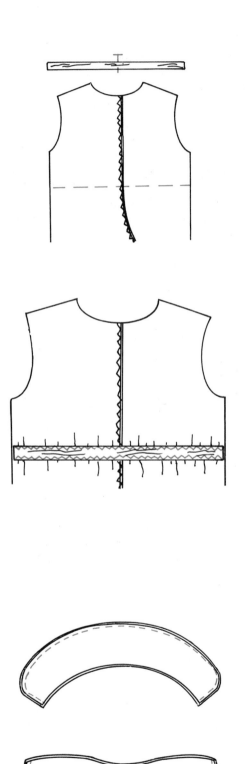

ELASTIC AT BACK WAIST

If desired, you can add elastic to the back waistline. Use ¾" (2 cm) wide elastic. Cut the elastic half of the child's waist measurement. Mark the waistline on the back of the jumpsuit. Divide the elastic in half with a pin. Pin the elastic to the wrong side of the back with the pin in the elastic at the center back seam. Place the middle of the elastic on the marked line. Sew on both sides of the elastic, stretching the elastic to fit the fabric.

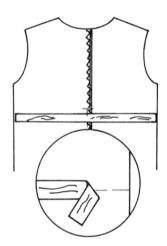

Sew the front to the back at the shoulder seams.

If you are using the rounded collar, place the collar pieces, right sides together, and stitch around the edges, leaving the neckline open. Turn the collar right side out and press.

If you are using the pointed collar, fold the collar double lengthwise, right sides together, and sew the ends. Turn right side out and press.

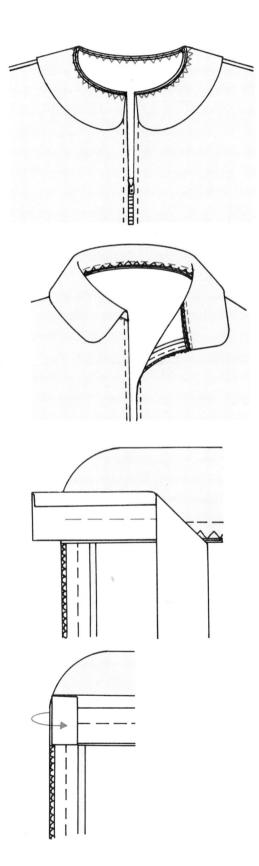

There are different ways you can sew on the collar. The fastest way is to match the center back of the collar to the center back of the neckline, the dots on collar to the shoulder seams and ends of the collar to the center front. Make sure that the undercollar is placed on the right side of the neckline. Sew on the collar through all layers using a ¼'' (6 mm) seam allowance.

With the seam allowance toward the garment, sew through seam allowance and garment close to the neckline seam.

If you want to hide the seam allowance around the neck opening, it can be done using bias tape. Unfold one edge of the bias tape and pin this edge to the collar with the raw edges together. Sew using a ¼'' (6 mm) seam allowance. Fold under the ends of the tape. Turn the tape over the seam allowance and topstitch close to the folded inner edge of tape.

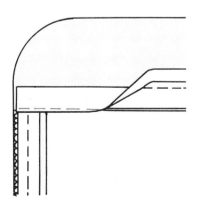

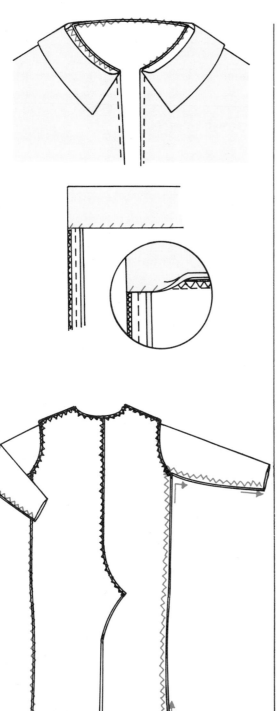

Another method of sewing on the collar is to pin one layer of the collar to the neck opening, placing the under collar on the right side of the neckline. Match the center back dots on the collar to the shoulder seam and the ends of the collar to the center front. Sew on the under collar.

Press the seam allowance into the collar. Fold under the seam allowance of the upper collar and attach it by hand.

Sew in the sleeves by matching the dot on the cap of the sleeve to the shoulder seam and underarm edges.

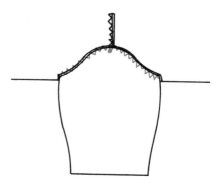

Starting at the bottom of the jumpsuit, sew the side seam and sleeve seam in one continuous operation.

INSIDE LEG SEAMS WITHOUT SNAPS

Line up the inside leg seam, matching the bottom edge and the crotch. Start sewing from the bottom of one leg up to the crotch, stop here. Sew the other leg in the same way. Hem the legs and the sleeves either by machine or by hand.

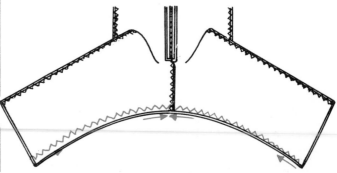

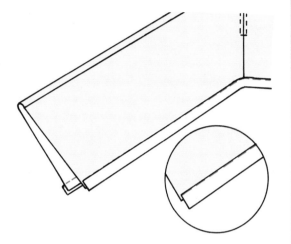

INSIDE LEG SEAMS WITH SNAPS

If you plan to use snaps on the inside leg seams, check to make sure you have added ½″ (1.3 cm) to the width of the inside leg seam.

We suggest that you use single fold bias tape to finish the leg and crotch openings. Cut two lengths of ½″ (1.3 cm) wide bias tape the same length as the inside leg seams, measured from the bottom of one leg to the bottom of the other leg.

Overlap the wrong side of the tape on the right side of the leg openings ¼″ (6 mm). Sew a seam close to the edge of the tape. Fold the bias tape to the wrong side. Sew a second seam on the other edge of the tape.

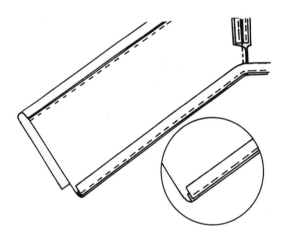

Hem the legs at the desired length. Attach snaps at the leg opening. The number of snaps will depend upon the length of the legs.

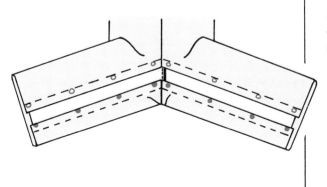

JUMPSUITS VARIATIONS

A jumpsuit can look very attractive by making use of a neckband instead of a collar. To obtain the correct length of the band, measure the neckline. Cut the band 2½" (6.5 cm) wide with the stretch of the fabric lengthwise.

Fold the fabric double, lengthwise, right side to right side, and sew a seam across each end. You can sew it straight across or round off the top edge as illustrated. Turn the band right side out. Divide the band in half and mark with a pin.

Place the band right side to right side along the neck opening, matching the pin to the center back and the ends of the band at the center front. Sew on the band through all layers, using ¼" (6 mm) seam allowance.

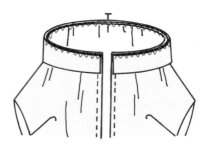

Another method of sewing on the band so that the raw edges will not show at the neckline is to sew only one edge of the band to the right side of the neckline. On the inside, fold under the raw edges of the band and stitch it in place by hand.

Instead of just hemming the sleeves, it looks very attractive to use cuffs (see Section II).

SIDE TABS

A very attractive variation can be added to the jumpsuit by adding tabs to the side seams. You have to sew on the tab before you sew the side seams.

Cut two pieces of fabric 4'' (10 cm) wide and 4½'' (11 cm) long for Sizes 1 and 2 and 4¾'' (12 cm) long for Sizes 3 and 4.

Fold the tabs, right sides together, and sew the long edge and one end. The front ends of the tabs can be straight or rounded. See illustration. Turn the tabs right side out and press.

Pin the tabs to each side of the front of the jumpsuit above the waistline, placing the raw edges of the tab along the edges of the side seams. Sew across to keep the tab in place.

Sew on a button through the tab and the front to keep in place.

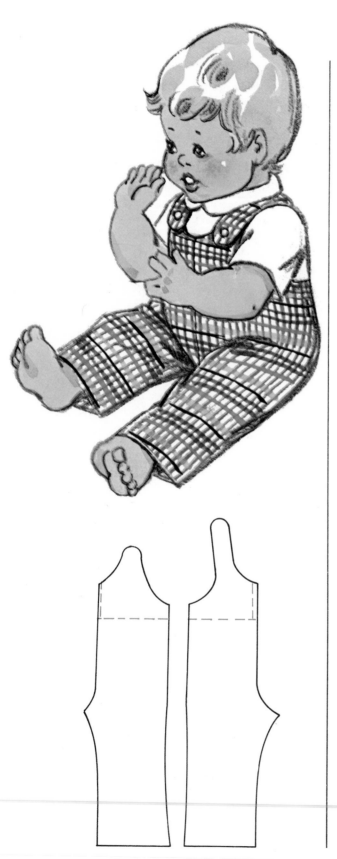

COVERALL

Actually, a coverall is really a jumpsuit without the sleeves and the collar. Use Master Pattern Piece No. 1 for the front and No. 2 for the back, follow cutting line B for the neckline and arm opening. This is a practical garment and is very good looking when worn over a T-shirt. The neckline and arm opening can be finished with facing or bias tape.

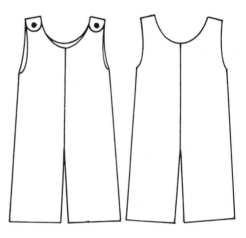

COVERALLS WITH FACING

The Master Pattern does not include any facing pieces. To make a facing, measure down 2″ (5 cm) underneath the arm opening and draw a line across the back and front pattern pieces. Trace the upper portion of the pattern down to this line. Eliminate the seam allowance at the center front and the center back. When cutting out the facing, place the center back and the center front on the fold.

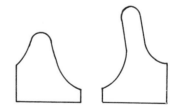

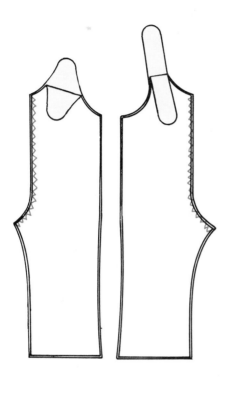

If you want to have snaps on the inside leg seams to make it easier to change diapers, refer to the jumpsuit.

Place the front pieces, right side to right side, and sew the center front seam. Place the back pieces, right side to right side, and sew the center back seam.

Place the back and front facing on the back and front of the coveralls, right side to right side. Match all raw edges around the neck and arm openings. Sew on the facing. Clip the curved seam allowance. Turn the facing to the inside and press.

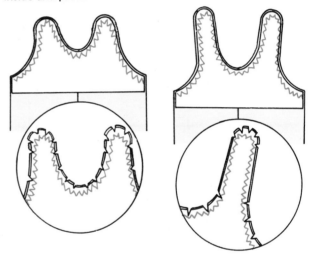

Place the back and front of the coverall, right side to right side, and sew the side seams and the facing, starting at the bottom edge of the leg, sew to the edge of the facing.

Turn the facing to the wrong side. You can either press down the edges around the neck and arm openings, top-stitch around these openings, or, if you have a sewing machine with decorative stitches, this is an excellent place to use one of these stitches.

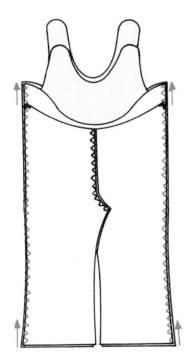

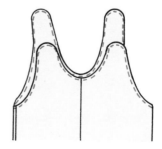

61

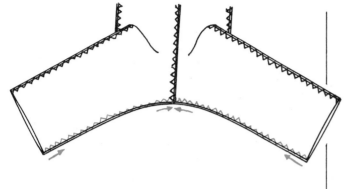

Sew the inside leg seams. If you want to have snaps on the inside leg seams, refer to the instructions given for the jumpsuit.

Hem the bottom of the legs.

Make a vertical buttonhole on the back of each tab. Sew on the buttons on the front tabs to match the buttonholes.

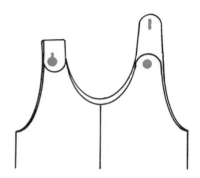

So that the coverall will fit the child for a longer period, you can increase the length of the front tab when you cut out the coverall. Move the location of the button as the child grows.

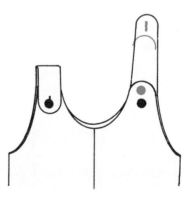

If the legs start to get too short and the body still fits, you can cut off the legs, hem them and you have a very attractive, short leg coverall. A coverall with short legs and without a T-shirt makes a perfect sunsuit. For variation, you can add a couple of pockets.

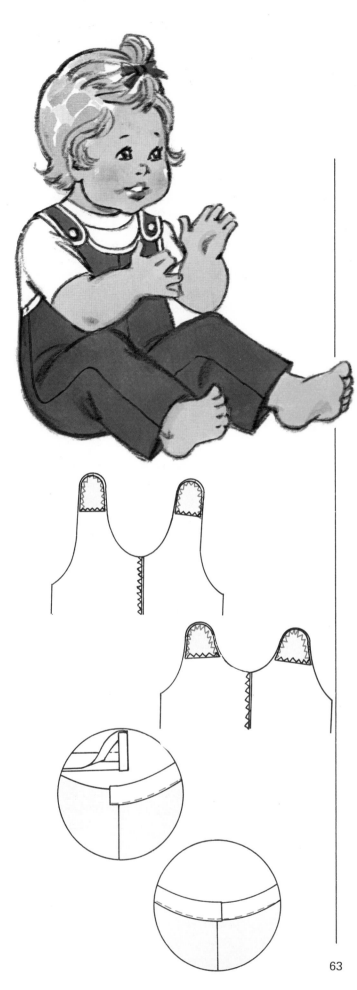

COVERALLS FINISHED WITH BIAS TAPE

Instead of using facing for the arm and neck opening, you can finish these edges by using bias tape. In this case, you need a facing only on the tabs where you plan to have a button and buttonhole. Measure from the top of the tab 2½" (6 cm) down on the back and 2" (5 cm) on the front and trace only that part.

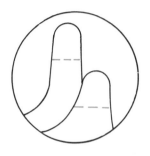

Start by overcasting the inner edge of the tab facings. Pin the tab facings to the shoulder tabs, wrong sides together. Sew around the outer edges to keep the facing in place.

Apply the bias tape to the neck and the arm openings starting at the center back. Insert the raw edges of the neck and the arm openings into the fold of the bias tape. The narrow edge of the tape is to the right side. Topstitch through all layers from the right side, continuing all the way around to the center back. Finish the end of the bias tape by folding the end under and continue topstitching.

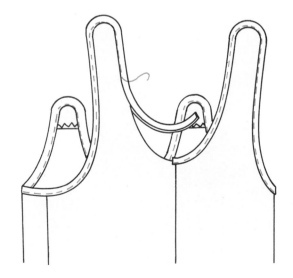

If you would like to make an applique or monogram for the jumpsuit or coverall, see Section VI.

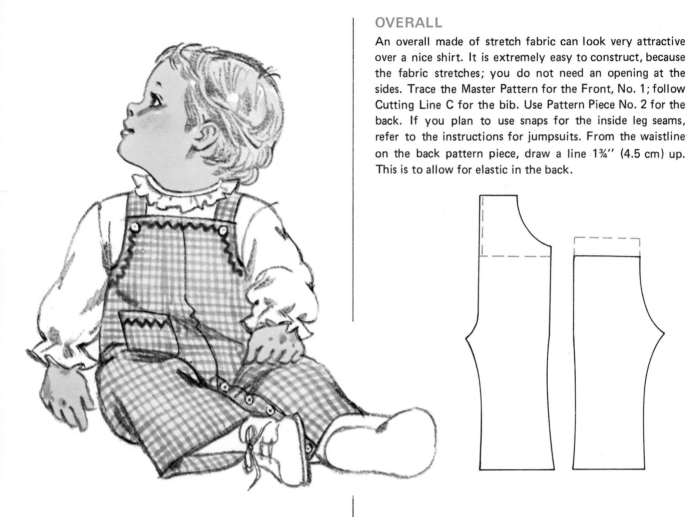

OVERALL

An overall made of stretch fabric can look very attractive over a nice shirt. It is extremely easy to construct, because the fabric stretches; you do not need an opening at the sides. Trace the Master Pattern for the Front, No. 1; follow Cutting Line C for the bib. Use Pattern Piece No. 2 for the back. If you plan to use snaps for the inside leg seams, refer to the instructions for jumpsuits. From the waistline on the back pattern piece, draw a line 1¾'' (4.5 cm) up. This is to allow for elastic in the back.

For a front facing for the bib, trace off the upper part of the front pattern down to the waist. Eliminate the seam allowance at the center front. When cutting out the facing, place the facing on a fold.

For the shoulder straps, cut two bands 2¾'' (7 cm) wide and the approximate length for Size 1T is 16½'' (42 cm); 2T is 17'' (43 cm); 3T is 17½'' (45 cm); 4T is 18'' (46 cm).

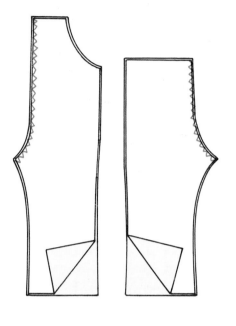

Cut out the pattern pieces. The overall can be made with either short or long legs. Start sewing the center front and the center back seams. Place the facing for the bib, right side to right side, on the bib with the raw edges together. Sew around the bib except at the side seams. Trim the corners, turn the facing to the inside and press.

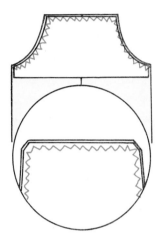

Pin the front to the back, right sides together, at the outside leg seam. The top edge of the back should be even with the edge of the front facing. Sew from the bottom edge of the leg to the top edge of the back.

Turn the top edge of the back 1" (2.5 cm) to the wrong side and press. Sew a seam ¼" (6 mm) from the raw edge to form the casing for the elastic.

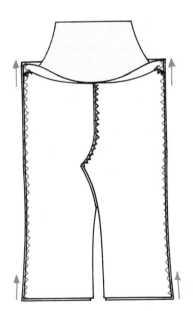

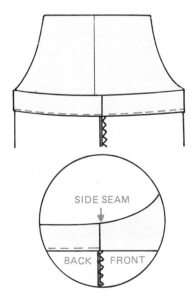

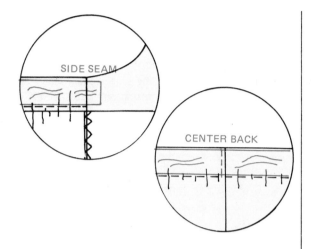

Cut a piece of ¾″ (2 cm) wide elastic for the back. The length is one-half of the waist measurement less 2″ (5 cm).

Thread the elastic into the back casing, extend the elastic ¼″ (6 mm) on each side seam. On the right side, sew across the casing very close to the side seam to secure the elastic. Sew across the casing at the center back to keep the elastic from rolling. Sew the inside leg seams or finish the inside leg seams with snaps.

Fold the fabric for the shoulder straps, right side to right side, lengthwise. Sew one long side and one short side on each strap. Turn the straps right side out.

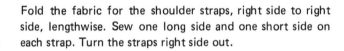

Attach the unfinished ends of the straps to the inside of the coverall, half-way between the side seam and the center back. Sew a seam across the straps at the top and bottom of the elastic. Make two buttonholes on the top of the bib. At the correct spot, sew a button on each strap. Hem the legs.

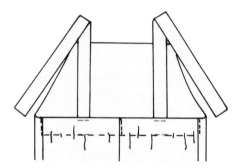

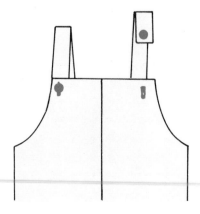

KNIT PULL-ON PANTS AND SHORTS

Pull-on pants and shorts are excellent garments for toddlers who are interested in trying to dress or undress themselves. They are easy to both take off and put on. To coordinate an outfit, save a scrap of fabric from the pants and use it to make an attractive applique on a shirt that will be worn with the pants (see Section VI).

Trace off the Master Pattern No. 2 for the back and No. 1 for the front. When tracing, add 1¾″ (4.5 cm) up from the waist to allow for the elastic. Cut out the pattern.

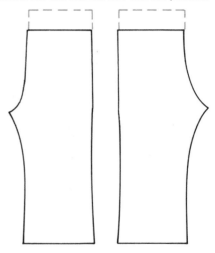

Sew the side seams starting at the bottom of the legs up to the waist. Now sew the inside leg seams, again starting from the bottom of the legs up to the crotch.

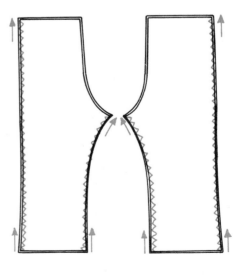

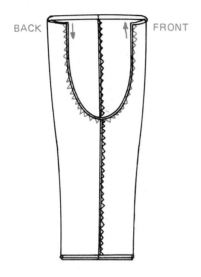

BACK   FRONT

Place one leg inside the other leg, right side to right side. Pin the crotch matching the inside leg seams and the waist. Sew the crotch seam starting at the back waist all the way around to the front waist.

At the waistline, press 1″ (2.5 cm) to the wrong side to form a casing.

We recommend using ¾″ (2 cm) wide elastic for the waist. Measure the elastic exactly the same length as the child's waist measurement; or you may want to use the following approximate measurements for the waist.

T1	20″	(51 cm)
T2	20½″	(52 cm)
T3	21″	(53 cm)
T4	21½″	(54 cm)

Overlap, and sew the ends of the elastic together to form a circle.

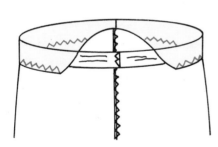

Place the elastic inside the casing and sew all the way around. Be careful that you do not sew through the elastic.

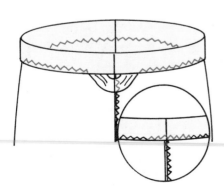

Another method is to sew the casing first, leaving a 1″ (2.5 cm) opening for inserting the elastic. Pull the elastic through the opening and sew the ends together. Close the opening.

Hem the slacks or shorts at the desired length.

Press the creases by lining up the inside and outside seams up to the knees. Above the knees, press the crease by following the grain line.

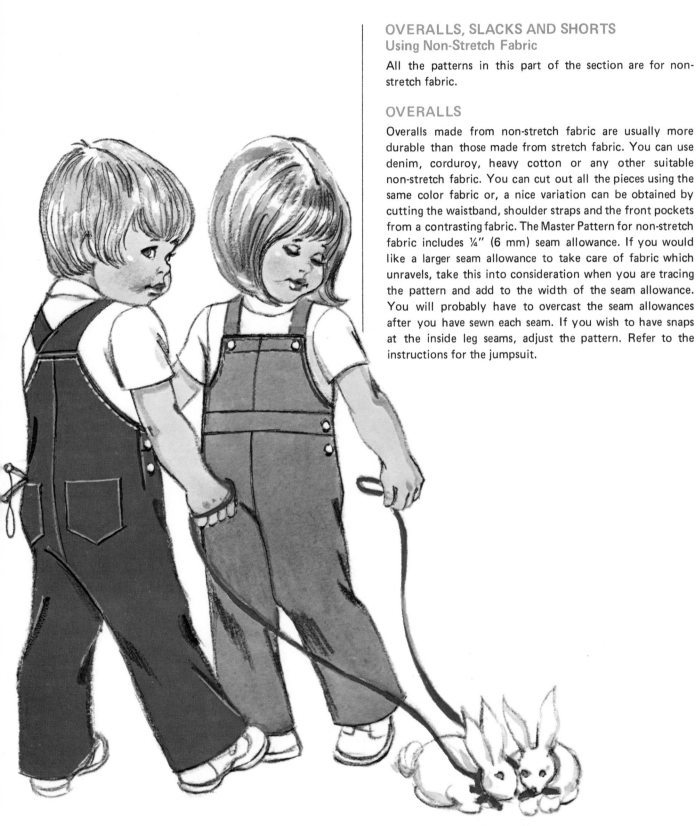

OVERALLS, SLACKS AND SHORTS
Using Non-Stretch Fabric

All the patterns in this part of the section are for non-stretch fabric.

OVERALLS

Overalls made from non-stretch fabric are usually more durable than those made from stretch fabric. You can use denim, corduroy, heavy cotton or any other suitable non-stretch fabric. You can cut out all the pieces using the same color fabric or, a nice variation can be obtained by cutting the waistband, shoulder straps and the front pockets from a contrasting fabric. The Master Pattern for non-stretch fabric includes ¼" (6 mm) seam allowance. If you would like a larger seam allowance to take care of fabric which unravels, take this into consideration when you are tracing the pattern and add to the width of the seam allowance. You will probably have to overcast the seam allowances after you have sewn each seam. If you wish to have snaps at the inside leg seams, adjust the pattern. Refer to the instructions for the jumpsuit.

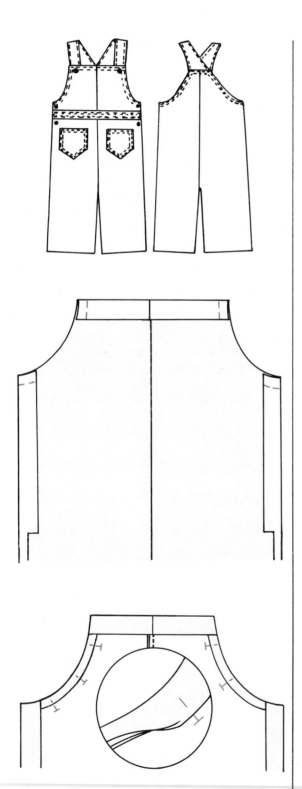

Trace off the Master Pattern Piece No. 19 for the front and 20 for the back. Use Pattern Piece No. 21 for the shoulder strap. Waistband - 23; back pocket - 25.

Cut out the pattern pieces. Sew the center back and center front seams.

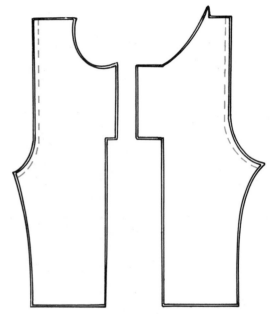

At the top of the bib, fold the fabric on the folding line to the right side. Sew the short ends using ½" (1.3 cm) seam allowance. Turn the facing to the wrong side. Turn the side seam extensions on the mark on pattern towards the right side. Sew across the extension using ½" (1.3 cm) seam allowance. Turn the extension toward the wrong side. Fold a hem at the arm opening between the facings, fold under the raw edges. Topstitch the bib on the front, close to the edge. Sew a second seam ¼" (6 mm) in from the first seam.

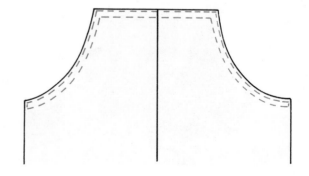

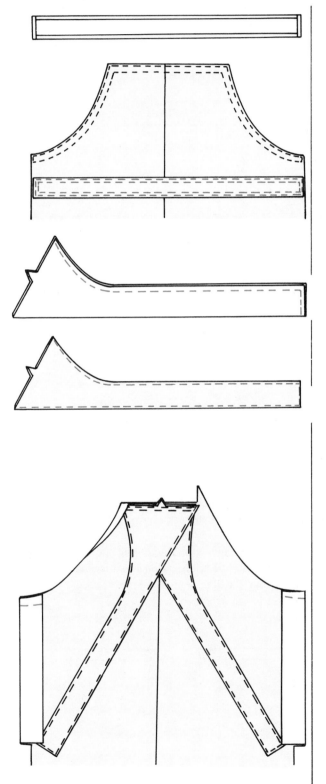

Press the raw edges of the waistband ¼'' (6 mm) to the wrong side. Place the waistband across the front 1'' (2.5 cm) down from the arm opening, and edge to edge with the sides. Sew around the band close to the edge and then sew another seam ¼'' (6 mm) in from the first seam.

Fold the two shoulder straps double lengthwise, right side to right side. Sew across the short end and the long side leaving the wide end open. Turn the straps right side out. Topstitch around the straps close to the edges. Place the straps on top of each other, placing the raw edges together and matching the notches. Sew a seam across to keep them in place. Place the straps right side to right side, on the top edge of the back of the overall. Sew across using ¼'' (6 mm) seam allowance. Fold the side extensions on the folding line towards the right side; sew across the extension at the arm opening using ½'' (1.3 cm) seam allowance. Turn the extension to the wrong side.

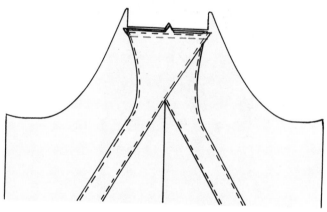

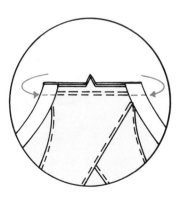

Fold a hem on the arm opening to the wrong side. Fold under the raw edges. Topstitch, close to the edge around the arm openings and across the shoulder straps. Sew another seam ¼'' (6 mm) in.

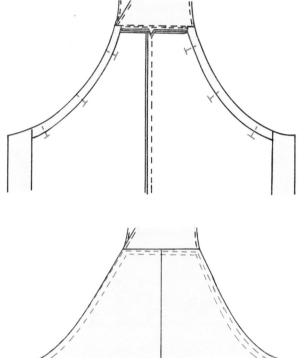

If you plan to have pockets either in front or in back, now is the time to make pockets.

Fold the top of the pocket on the folding line to the wrong side and topstitch close to the fold. Sew a second seam ¼'' (6 mm) in from the first seam. Press the seam allowances of the pocket to the wrong side.

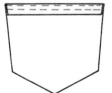

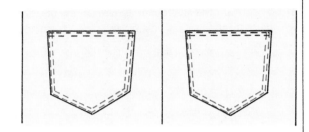

Pin the pockets in position. Sew on the pockets close to the folded edge. Sew a second seam ¼″ (6 mm) in from the first seam.

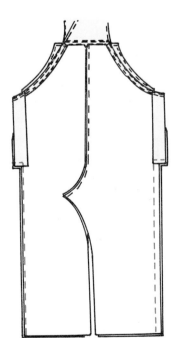

Press the extended facing on back side seam at the folding line towards the wrong side. Sew the side seam starting at the bottom up to the the side extension, sew across the bottom of the extension. Sew the inside leg seams, starting from the bottom of each leg to the crotch. If you plan to use snaps for the inside leg seams, follow the instructions for the jumpsuit.

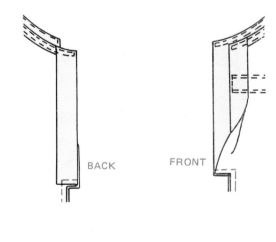

BACK   FRONT

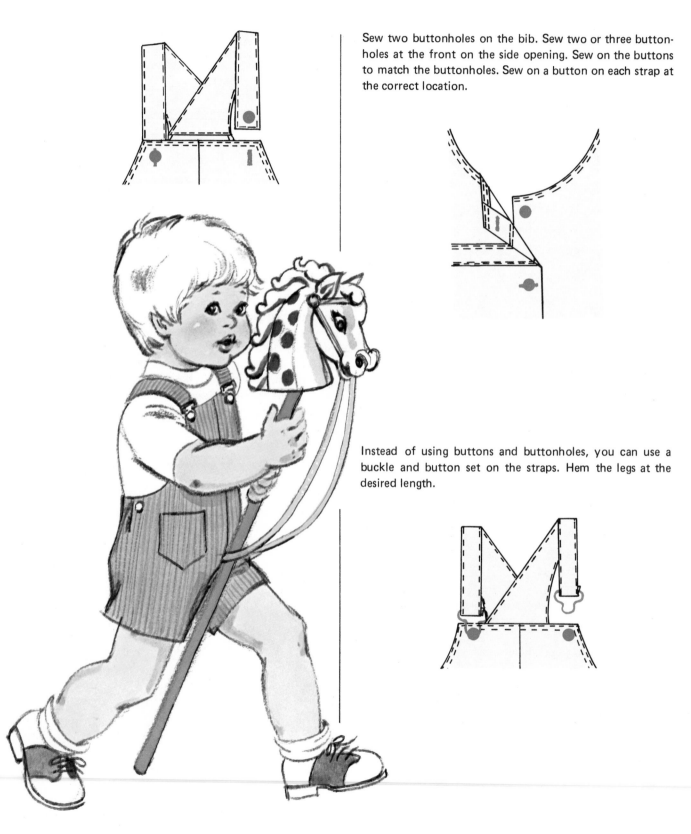

Sew two buttonholes on the bib. Sew two or three buttonholes at the front on the side opening. Sew on the buttons to match the buttonholes. Sew on a button on each strap at the correct location.

Instead of using buttons and buttonholes, you can use a buckle and button set on the straps. Hem the legs at the desired length.

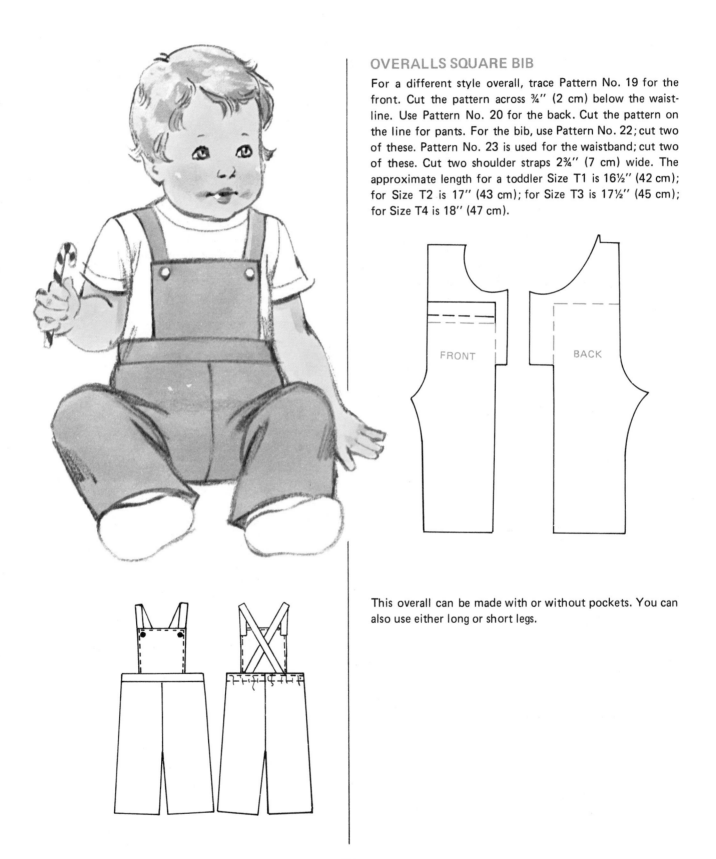

OVERALLS SQUARE BIB

For a different style overall, trace Pattern No. 19 for the front. Cut the pattern across ¾″ (2 cm) below the waistline. Use Pattern No. 20 for the back. Cut the pattern on the line for pants. For the bib, use Pattern No. 22; cut two of these. Pattern No. 23 is used for the waistband; cut two of these. Cut two shoulder straps 2¾″ (7 cm) wide. The approximate length for a toddler Size T1 is 16½″ (42 cm); for Size T2 is 17″ (43 cm); for Size T3 is 17½″ (45 cm); for Size T4 is 18″ (47 cm).

FRONT

BACK

This overall can be made with or without pockets. You can also use either long or short legs.

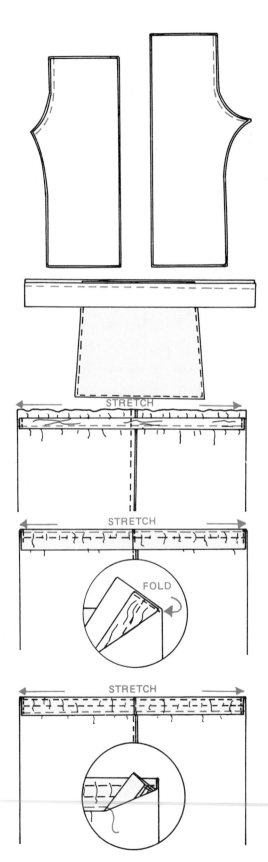

Cut out pattern pieces. Sew the center front and the center back seam. Place the two bib pieces, right side to right side. Sew around on three sides, leaving the bottom edge open. Trim the corners. Turn the bib right side out. Topstitch around the three sides ¼" (6 mm) in from the edge.

Place the bib on the right side of one of the waistbands. The center of the bib should be at the center of the waistband and should be edge to edge with the band. Place the other waistband on top of the first waistband, right side to right side. Sew a seam along the waistband to attach the bib to the waistband. Turn the waistband right side out. Attach the waistband to the front of the pants by placing one edge of the waistband, right side to right side, with the top of the pants. Sew a seam across.

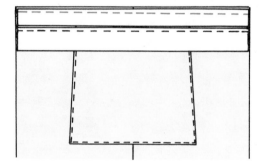

For the back, you need ¾" (2 cm) wide elastic. The length should be one half of the waist measurement less 2" (5 cm). Divide the elastic in half with a pin. Pin the elastic to the wrong side of the back waist, placing the top edge of elastic ½" (1.3 cm) down from the top edge. Match the pin in the elastic to the center back. The ends of the elastic should be even with the side edges. Stitch across the width of the elastic at the center back and at the side seams ¼" (6 mm) from the raw edges. Sew the elastic to the back by sewing a seam in the middle of the elastic, stretching the elastic to fit the back.

Fold the top edge of the back along the bottom edge of the elastic to the inside. Sew through all layers ¼" (6 mm) from the top edge, stretching the elastic to fit the back. Fold the seam allowance under the elastic and sew ¼" (6 mm) from the bottom edge of the elastic through all the layers, stretching the elastic to fit the back.

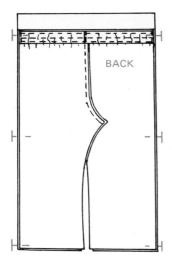

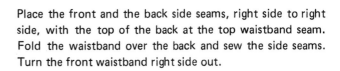

Place the front and the back side seams, right side to right side, with the top of the back at the top waistband seam. Fold the waistband over the back and sew the side seams. Turn the front waistband right side out.

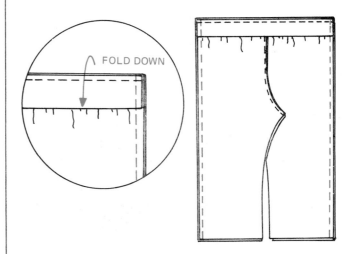

FOLD DOWN

On the right side, sew a seam as close as possible to the waistband seam to attach the inside waistband. Sew the inside leg seams.

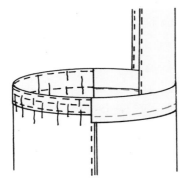

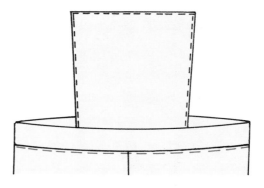

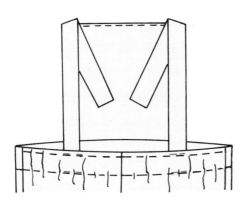

Fold the shoulder straps lengthwise, right side to right side, and sew the long side and one short side. Turn the straps right side out. Pin the shoulder straps to the inside of the back waist in the middle between the center back seam and the side seam. Sew at the top of the waist and in the same line of stitches as the casing seam. Make buttonholes on top edge of bib, sew on buttons to end of straps.

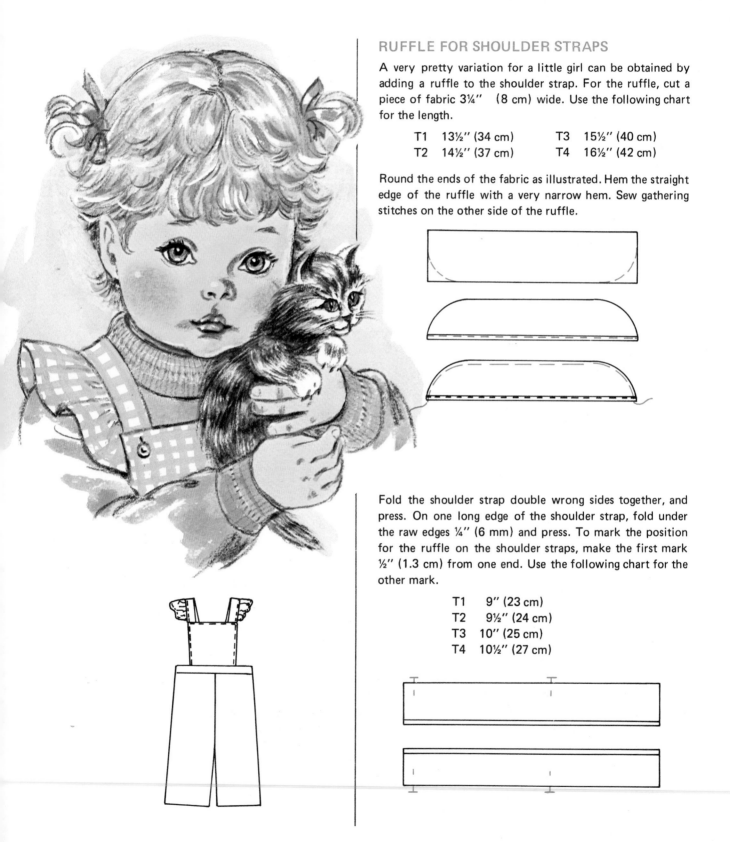

RUFFLE FOR SHOULDER STRAPS

A very pretty variation for a little girl can be obtained by adding a ruffle to the shoulder strap. For the ruffle, cut a piece of fabric 3¼" (8 cm) wide. Use the following chart for the length.

T1	13½" (34 cm)	T3	15½" (40 cm)
T2	14½" (37 cm)	T4	16½" (42 cm)

Round the ends of the fabric as illustrated. Hem the straight edge of the ruffle with a very narrow hem. Sew gathering stitches on the other side of the ruffle.

Fold the shoulder strap double wrong sides together, and press. On one long edge of the shoulder strap, fold under the raw edges ¼" (6 mm) and press. To mark the position for the ruffle on the shoulder straps, make the first mark ½" (1.3 cm) from one end. Use the following chart for the other mark.

T1	9" (23 cm)
T2	9½" (24 cm)
T3	10" (25 cm)
T4	10½" (27 cm)

Pin the wrong side of the ruffle to the right side of the shoulder strap on the unpressed side, placing the ruffle between the marks on the shoulder straps. Pull the gathering stitches so that the ruffle fits the strap. Adjust the gathers so that they are even. Sew on top of the gathering stitches. Fold the ends of the shoulder strap double, right sides together, and sew the ends. Turn right side out.

Fold the folded edge of the strap over the seam allowance, covering the stitching with the ruffle extending. Topstitch close to the folded edge of the straps.

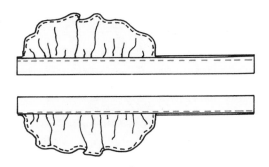

PULL-ON PANTS

For pull-on pants with elastic in the back and a waistband in the front, trace pattern No. 19 for the front, cut across ¾'' (2 cm) below the waistline. For the back, use pattern No. 20 and cut on the pants line. For the waistband, use pattern No. 24. Cut one. You need one piece of elastic ¾'' (2 cm) wide. The length should be one-half of the waist measurement less 2'' (5 cm). You can make these pants with long or short legs and with or without pockets. Start out by sewing the center front and the center back seam. Place the front waistband, right side to right side, on the top edge of the pants. Sew a seam across it.

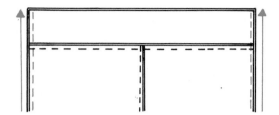

Sewing the elastic across the back and sewing the side seam and the inside leg seam is the same as described for a square bib overall.

PULL-ON PANTS WITH ELASTIC AROUND THE WAIST

Use pattern No. 19 for the front and cut on the pants line. For the back, use pattern No. 20. Also cut on the pants line. For the waist, use ¾" (2 cm) elastic and cut the elastic the same size as the child's waist. Sew the center front, center back, side seams and inside leg seams.

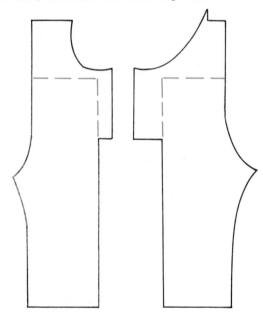

Fold the top edge of the pants 1¼" (3.2 cm) to the wrong side. Fold under the raw edges and sew around the waist, leaving a 1" (2.5 cm) opening to insert the elastic. Insert the elastic through the opening and sew the ends together. Close the opening. Hem the bottom of the legs.

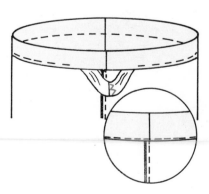

dresses

It is a fact that most little girls tend to spend most of their time in T-shirts with either shorts or slacks. There are times, however, when an attractive little dress is very appropriate. At this age, most little girls like to get dressed up. Dresses are fun to make and you can use your imagination to create a truly one-of-a-kind dress by using lace, trim, appliques, etc. You can use almost any lightweight fabric, cotton or blend of cotton and other fibers, just as long as the fabric is easy to care for. If the dress requires more than usual care in washing or extensive ironing, you may find that you will not use the dress as often as you should.

BASIC DRESS

Included with this book is a pattern for a basic dress. We will first explain how to construct this basic dress and this will be followed with a number of ideas on how the basic dress can be changed to give you a wide variety of styles. You can use the pattern to create dresses for special occasions such as a party dress, Christmas dress, Easter dress, etc. As a toddler's underpants often show, it is a good idea to use the same fabric for the underpants as you use for the dress.

For the basic dress, use Master Pattern No. 15 for the front bodice. For the back bodice, use No. 16. For the sleeves, use No. 17; the sleeves can be either long or short. For the collar, use No. 18. There is no pattern piece for the back and front skirt. For the skirt, cut 2 pieces of fabric using the following scale. This includes a 2" (5 cm) hem.

	Length	Width
T1	11¼" (28.5cm)	23" (58.5cm)
T2	11 7/8" (30cm)	24" (61cm)
T3	12½" (32cm)	25" (63.5cm)
T4	13 1/8" (33cm)	26" (66cm)

The pattern includes a 5/8" (1.5cm) seam allowance. This is the best seam allowance to use when making the dress using non-stretch fabric. If you are using stretch fabric, the seam allowances should be trimmed to ¼" (6 mm) after sewing each seam and the seam allowances overcasted together.

Cut out the pattern pieces. For the opening in the back, fold under the raw edges of the facing ¼" (6 mm) to the wrong side and stitch. Press facing on the folding line to the wrong side. Sew the shoulder seams and the side seams with right side to right side.

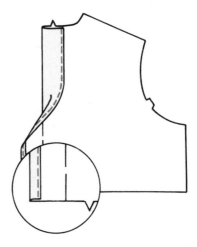

Place the collars right side to right side and sew around the outer edge, leaving the neckline open. Clip and trim the seam allowances. Turn the collars right side out and press. Stitch the collar together at the center front with a few stitches by hand on the seam allowance.

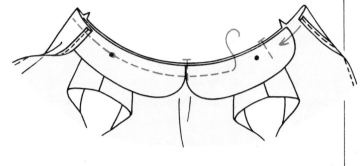

Mark the center front of the dress. Pin the collars on the right side of the neckline with the ends of the collars at the center front. The other ends of the collars should end at the center back.

Fold the back facing on the folding line to the right side over the collar. Sew on the collar through all layers, including the facing in the seam. Trim neckline seam allowance to ¼'' (6 mm).

The raw edges of the neckline can be covered with self-fabric or bias tape. For bias tape, follow the procedures described in the Jumpsuit Section III.

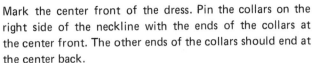

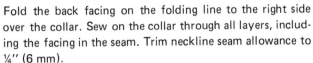

Instead of using bias tape to cover the raw edges, you may use self-fabric. Cut a strip of fabric on the bias the length of the neckline and 1¼'' (3.2cm) wide. Fold the strip double, lengthwise, wrong sides together. Place the strip on the collar with the raw edges of the strip and the collar together. Sew the strip to the collar on the same stitching line as used to sew on the collar from center back to center back. Cut off excess length of bias strip. Fold the facing to the wrong side and fold the strip over the seam allowance. To keep the strip in place, topstitch close to the folded edge.

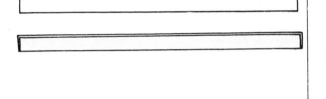

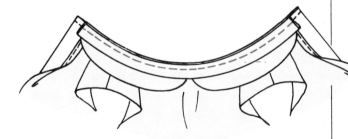

If you do not wish to cover up the raw edges with bias tape or self-fabric, you can simply understitch the seam allowance to the neck opening.

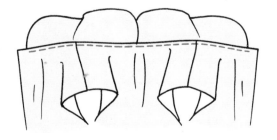

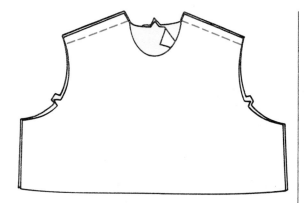

DOUBLE BODICE:

If you are using a very lightweight fabric, you can make the front and back bodice with a double layer of fabric. This will produce a neater appearance on the inside. To accomplish this, cut two layers of front and back.

Sew the shoulder seams for both layers. Make the collar as previously described.

Place the pieces, right side to right side, sandwiching the collar between the pieces with one end of the collar at the center front and the other end of the collar at the center back. Sew the collar in place.

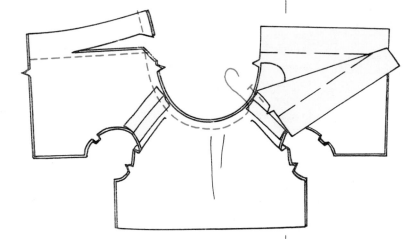

At the center back, sew a seam on the folding line. Trim the neckline seam allowance and trim back facing to ¼'' (6 mm). Turn the bodice right side out.

If you wish, you may understitch the collar at the neckline.

Sew the side seams.

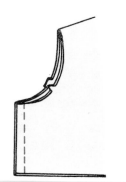

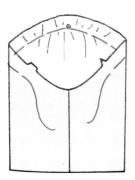

The Master Pattern calls for puffed sleeves. Start by sewing a gathering stitch on the cap of the sleeve between notches. Sew the sleeve seams and gather the top of the sleeve to fit the sleeve opening.

Sew on the sleeves by placing the center top of the cap at the shoulder seam. The sleeve seam should match the side seam. All of the gathering should be located on top of the sleeve. No gathering should be on the bottom of the sleeve. Trim the seam allowances to ¼'' (6 mm) and overcast.

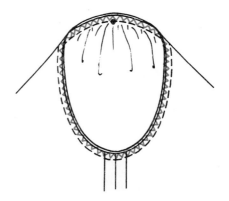

Sew the skirt seams, right side to right side. Sew two gathering stitches around the top of the skirt starting at one seam. Divide the top of the skirt in fourths with pins.

Overlap the left back of the bodice over the right back bodice matching the center back line. Sew a seam across the bottom of the opening to keep it in place. Divide the bodice of the dress in fourths with pins. Start from one side seam. Place the bodice of the dress and the skirt, right side to right side, matching the pins. The seams on the skirt should match with the side seams of the bodice. Gather the skirt between the pins to fit the bodice of the dress. Sew the skirt to the bodice using a 5/8'' (1.5 cm) seam allowance. Hem the skirt either by hand or machine to obtain the desired length.

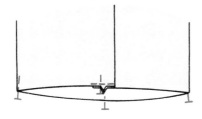

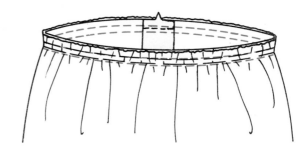

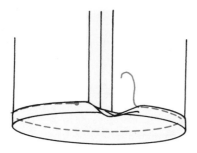

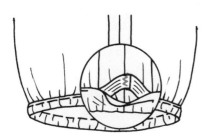

If you are using long or short sleeves, finish the sleeves in the same manner. Fold a 5/8'' (1.5 cm) wide hem towards the wrong side. Fold under the raw edges and sew close to the folded edge; leave an opening large enough to insert the elastic. Insert a narrow piece of elastic. To determine the length of the elastic, measure around the child's arm or wrist and add 1'' (2.5 cm). If you do not have the child's measurements, use the following chart.

Cut 2

Size	Long sleeves	Short sleeves
T1	5¼''(13.5cm)	7¼''(18.5cm)
T2	5½'' (14cm)	7½'' (19cm)
T3	5¾''(14.5cm)	7¾''(19.5cm)
T4	6'' (15cm)	8'' (20cm)

Overlap the ends of the elastic and secure them. Close the opening.

For the back of the dress, determine how many buttons you need. Make the buttonholes and sew on the buttons (see Section I).

VARIATION IN THE BASIC DRESS

BOW: A bow will greatly enhance a dress. Cut a strip of fabric 22″ (56 cm) long and 1″ (2.5 cm) wide. Fold the strip, right sides together, and sew a seam ¼″ (6 mm) from the folded edge. An easy way to turn this narrow strip is by using a bobby pin. Cut a small opening on the fold ½″ (1.3 cm) from one end of the strip. Insert a bobby pin with the smooth tips into the tie (hooked through the cut opening). Guide the bobby pin through the tie to the other end. See illustration. Make a knot at each end of the tie.

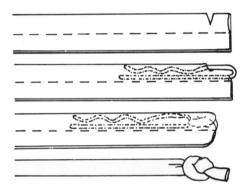

Tie a bow and attach it to the dress at the center front under the collar. If you do not want to make the bow, buy a piece of ribbon in a contrasting color and make a bow using the ribbon.

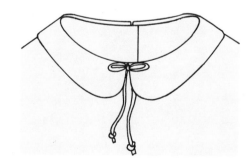

87

You do not necessarily have to place the bow at the collar. A bow also looks very attractive at the center front where the bodice and the skirt join. To add an extra touch, copy a pattern for a flower or a bell. Take two pieces of fabric, place them wrong side to wrong side. Between the layers of fabric, use fusible webbing and press. This will keep the two pieces of fabric together. Cut out the design.

Sew a zigzag seam around the edges to keep the fabric from unraveling. If you have made a flower, attach the flower to the end of the tie. To hide the stitches, attach a small button on top of the stitches which should be in the middle of the flower. If you are making a bell, simply attach the top of the bell to the tie.

BELT: A belt can be made using the same color as the dress or a coordinating color. Or the collar, sleeves and belt could be a contrasting color to the dress. Cut a strip of fabric 3¼″ (8 cm) wide and 53″ (135 cm) long. If you do not have a strip of fabric long enough, piece the belt 15″ (38 cm) from each end. This is to make the seams less noticeable.

The ends of the belt can be finished at an angle or straight across. Fold the belt double lengthwise, right sides together, and sew the ends and the long edge, leaving an opening for turning. Turn the belt right side out and press it. Close the opening.

As a little toddler has a tendency to pull on a belt, we suggest that you place the belt at the seam in front of the dress that connects the top to the bottom of the dress. Secure the belt at the side seams.

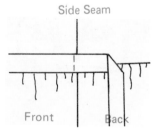

TIERED SKIRT: A tiered skirt usually has two tiers except for a long dress where you may want to add additional tiers according to how long the dress will be. If you are constructing a two tier skirt, cut the tiers using the following chart:

Cut 2 of Each

Size	T1	T2	T3	T4
Top Tier				
Length	5″ (13 cm)	5¼″(13.5cm)	5½″ (14cm)	5¾″(14.5cm)
Width	18¾″(47.5cm)	19½″(49.5cm)	20¼″(51.5cm)	21″(53 cm)
Bottom Tier (Includes a 2″ (5 cm) Hem)				
Length	7½″ (19 cm)	7 7/8″(20cm)	8¼″ (21 cm)	8 5/8″(22cm)
Width	26½″ (67cm)	27½″ (70cm)	28½″(72.5cm)	29½″ (75cm)

Place each tier, right side to right side, and sew the short sides. Sew two gathering seams on the top edge of each tier.

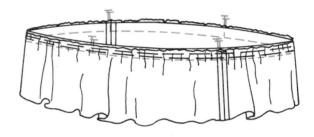

Divide the tops and the bottoms of the tiers in fourths with pins except for the bottom edge of the skirt. Start with the bottom tier, gather the top of the tier so that the pins match those at the bottom of the next tier. Sew the tiers together, right side to right side, using 5/8″ (1.5 cm) seam allowance. Gather the top tier to fit the bodice and sew them together. Hem the bottom of the skirt either by hand or by machine.

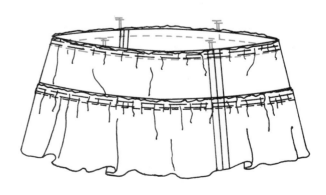

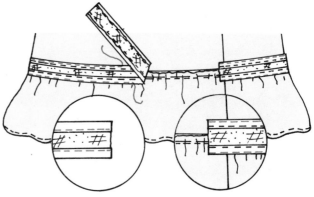

DECORATIVE BANDS: You may wish to add decorative bands where the tiers are joined together. This makes a very attractive party dress. Sew the tiers together, wrong side to wrong side, so that the seams are showing on the right side. Trim the seam allowance to ¼'' (6 mm). Place the band over the seam and sew on the band by sewing both edges.

Instead of a decorative band, you may use lace and trim. Sew a piece of trim to each side of the lace and then sew the trim and lace to the dress by sewing close to the outer edges of the trim.

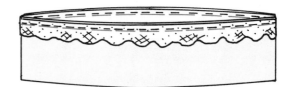

If you would like to have protruding lace or eyelets between the tiers, sew the lace or eyelets to the top of the tier and then gather the tier and lace or eyelet at the same time.

SKIRT WITH RUFFLES: To obtain the effect of a dress with two skirts when actually there is only one skirt, make a skirt with two ruffles, one ruffle is sewed to the bottom of the skirt, the other ruffle is sewed on top of the skirt above the bottom ruffle. Cut out the skirt and ruffles using the following chart:

Size	T1	T2	T3	T4
SKIRT				
Length	7 3/8"(19cm)	8" (20 cm)	8 5/8" (22cm)	9¼" (23.5 cm)
Width	23" (59 cm)	24" (61 cm)	25" (64 cm)	26" (66 cm)
BOTTOM RUFFLE - allows 3/8" (1 cm) for double narrow hem.				
Cut 2 - 3½"(9cm) Wide	34½" (87cm)	36" (92cm)	37½" (96 cm)	39" (99 cm)
TOP RUFFLE				
Cut 2 - 3" (7.5 cm) Wide	34½" (87 cm)	36" (92 cm)	37½" (96 cm)	39" (99 cm)

Sew on the bottom ruffle to the bottom edge of the skirt.

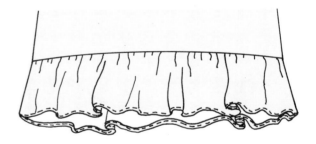

Sew the top ruffle together to form a circle. Fold a double narrow hem to the wrong side on both sides and sew the hem. Sew a gathering stitch on one long side approximately 5/8" (1.5 cm) from the edge.

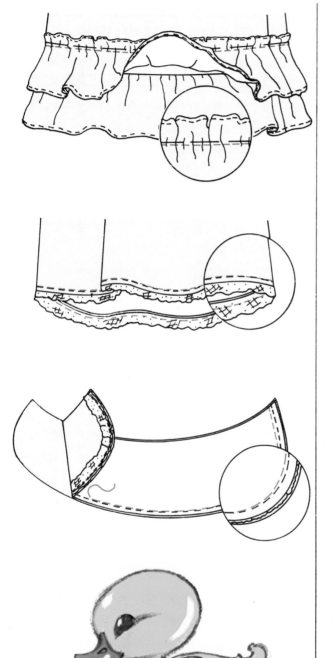

Gather the ruffle to fit the skirt. Place the ruffle 1½" (3.8 cm) above the ruffle. Sew it on to the skirt, using the same line as the gathering stitch. It is very attractive if you make the sleeves, collar and the bottom ruffle in one color and the bodice, skirt and top ruffle in another color.

LACE AT BOTTOM EDGE: If you would like to use lace or eyelet at the bottom of the dress, we suggest that you make a small hem on the bottom of the dress. Place the lace underneath the hem and sew on the lace using the same stitching line. You can use flat lace or eyelet, pregathered lace or eyelet, or, they may be gathered before sewing them on the dress.

COLLAR WITH LACE: We have described previously how to construct a collar. If you would like to alter the appearance of the dress, you can use a contrasting color for the collar or you can use lace on the edge. If you are using lace, cut two strips of lace one and a half times as long as the outer edge of the collars. Gather the lace so that it equals the outer edge of the collar. Sew on the lace to one collar. Place the collars right side to right side, sandwiching the lace between the collars with the raw edges together and stitch in the same line of stitching as for sewing on the lace.

Trim seam allowances. Turn the collar right side out and you have a very pretty lace edging.

Another pretty variation is to insert lace at the seam that connects the bodice to the skirt of the dress. If you do this, cut the lace one and a half times longer than the dress bodice seam. Gather the top of the skirt and the lace separately.

Place the lace on the right side of the dress bodice seam, raw edges together. Gather the lace to fit the bodice and sew on the lace. Place the right side of the bodice on the right side of the dress with the lace in between and sew through all layers.

LACE ON FRONT BODICE: You may also want to use vertical strips of lace on the front bodice. Lace can be gathered or flat. Sew as many rows as desired. See illustration.

For an even nicer effect, add a satin ribbon tie and add some lace at the bottom of the dress and sleeves.

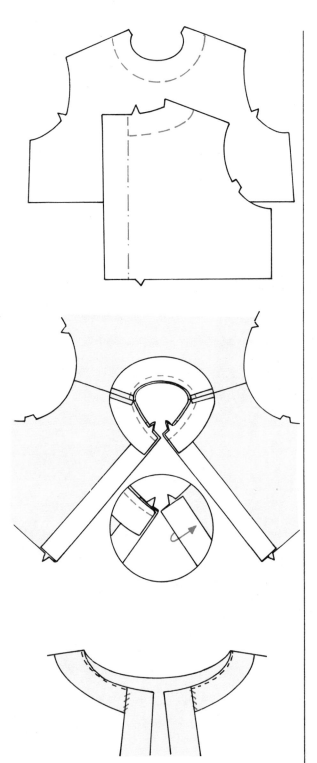

ROUND NECK: You may want to make a simple round neck instead of a collar. In this case, you will need a facing piece. Draw a line on the neckline on the back and front pattern piece. Measure down from the neckline 2" (5 cm) around both the back and the front neck opening with the back facing ending at the folding line. Trace off the facing pieces.

Sew the shoulder seam on the facing and the dress.

Fold the back facing on the folding line, right side to right side.

Place the facing, right side to right side, at the neckline with raw edges together. Sew the facing in place. Trim the seam allowances. Understitch the facing.

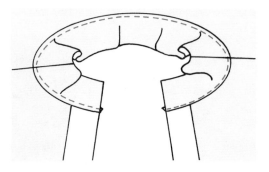

Fold the facing to the wrong side. Secure the ends of the back facing with a few hand stitches. You can topstitch around the neck opening with a regular straight stitch or you can use decorative stitches.

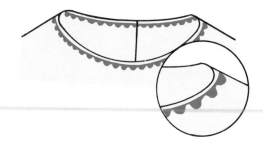

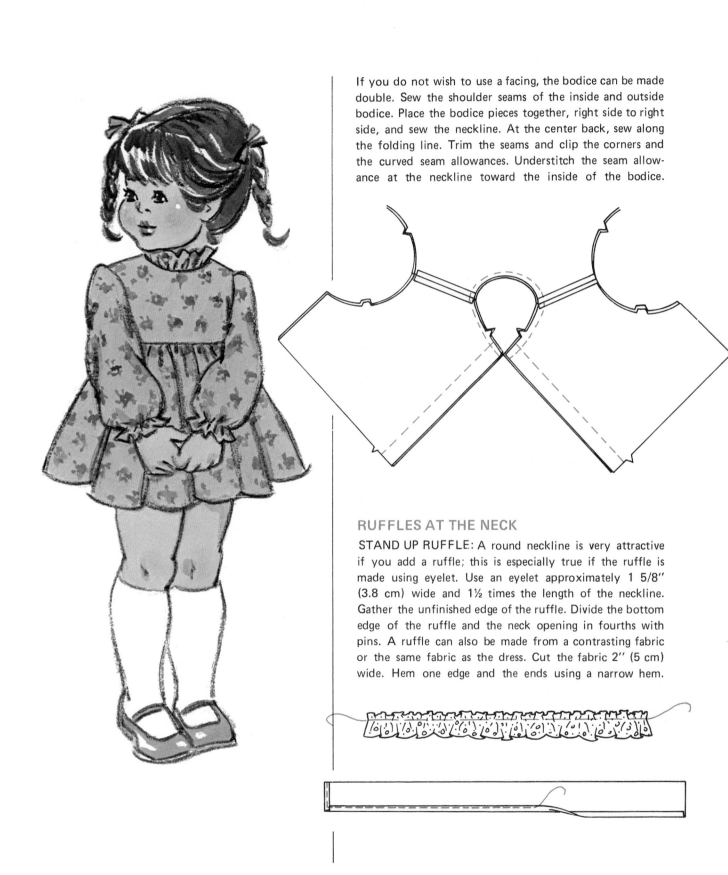

If you do not wish to use a facing, the bodice can be made double. Sew the shoulder seams of the inside and outside bodice. Place the bodice pieces together, right side to right side, and sew the neckline. At the center back, sew along the folding line. Trim the seams and clip the corners and the curved seam allowances. Understitch the seam allowance at the neckline toward the inside of the bodice.

RUFFLES AT THE NECK

STAND UP RUFFLE: A round neckline is very attractive if you add a ruffle; this is especially true if the ruffle is made using eyelet. Use an eyelet approximately 1 5/8" (3.8 cm) wide and 1½ times the length of the neckline. Gather the unfinished edge of the ruffle. Divide the bottom edge of the ruffle and the neck opening in fourths with pins. A ruffle can also be made from a contrasting fabric or the same fabric as the dress. Cut the fabric 2" (5 cm) wide. Hem one edge and the ends using a narrow hem.

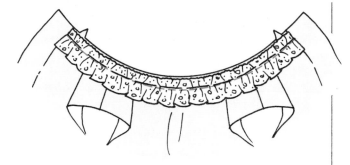

Pin the ruffle to the neckline with the right sides together, matching the pins; the ends of the ruffle should be at the folding line. Gather the ruffle by pulling the bobbin thread. Adjust the gathers evenly to fit the neckline. Sew on the ruffle on top of the gathering stitches. Trim the seam allowance to ¼'' (6 mm).

Finish the raw edges as previously described using either bias tape or self-fabric cut on the bias.

NECKLINE RUFFLE WITH BINDING: If you would like to have the type of ruffle which lies down, trim off the seam allowance around the neck opening.

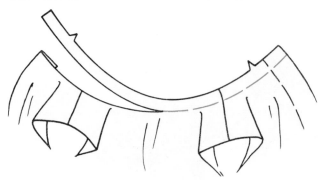

This type of ruffle can be made from lace eyelet or self-fabric. Cut the ruffle 1½ times the length of the neckline. Cut the self-fabric 1 5/8'' (4 cm) wide. If you are using lace or eyelet, cut it 1¼'' (3 cm) wide. If you are using self-fabric, hem one long side. If you wish, you can attach a narrow piece of lace at the bottom of the hem. Hem both short ends of the strip. Sew a gathering stitch on the unfinished long side. Divide the neck opening and the ruffle in fourths with pins.

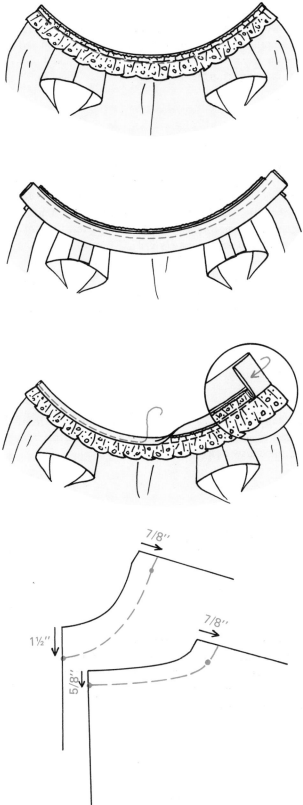

Place the wrong side of the ruffle on the right side of the neck opening, raw edges together, with the ends of the ruffle on the folding lines in the back. Match the pins and gather the ruffle to fit the neck opening. Sew on the ruffle using a ¼'' (6 mm) seam allowance.

We suggest that you finish the neckline with self-fabric binding. Cut a strip of fabric on the bias 2'' (5 cm) wide and the length of the neckline plus 1'' (2.5 cm). Fold the binding double lengthwise, wrong sides together. Pin the binding to the wrong side of the neckline with all the raw edges together. The binding should extend ½'' (1.3 cm) beyond the folding line in the back. Sew on the binding, using a ¼'' (6 mm) seam allowance.

Fold the binding over the raw edges toward the right side. Fold under the edges of the binding. Sew a straight stitch as close as possible to the fold.

If you prefer to have a deeper neckline when you use a ruffle, change the back and front pattern pieces as follows. At the center front, make a mark 1½'' (3.8 cm) down from the neck opening. Make a mark on the shoulder seam on both the front and back pattern piece 7/8'' (2 cm) in from the neck opening. At the center back, mark 5/8'' (1.5 cm) down from the neckline. Connect these marks with a smooth curved line as illustrated.

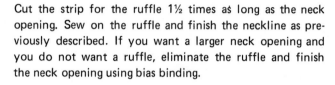

Cut the strip for the ruffle 1½ times as long as the neck opening. Sew on the ruffle and finish the neckline as previously described. If you want a larger neck opening and you do not want a ruffle, eliminate the ruffle and finish the neck opening using bias binding.

BODICE TUCKS AND TRIM

A very attractive front for a small toddler's dress can be made by using small tucks and trim. The tucks should be sewn before you cut out the front bodice. The reason for this is that the tucks will change the size of the bodice. We recommend small tucks between 1/8" (3 mm) to 1/4" (6 mm) wide and approximately 5/8" (1.5 cm) between the tucks. The easiest way to make tucks is to press the fabric, wrong side to wrong side at the point where the folded edge of the tuck is located. Sew six or eight tucks. Half the tucks should be pressed toward the right, the other half toward the left.

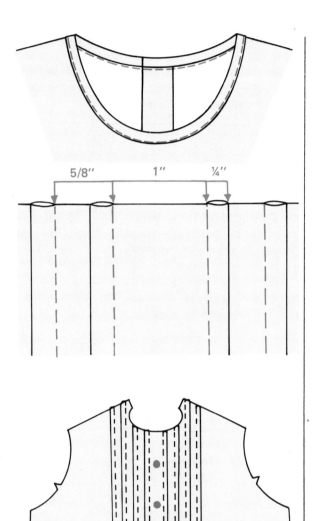

Cut out the front bodice making sure that the center front is halfway between the right and left tucks. Construct the dress as previously described.

Sew on a few pretty buttons on the center front between the rows of tucks.

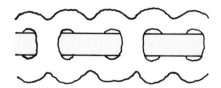

If you wish to frame the tucks, any pretty trim may be used. Or, you can use insertion lace. Take a narrow piece of colored ribbon the same width as the holes in the lace and thread the holes with the ribbon. You can either gather the lace or it can lay flat.

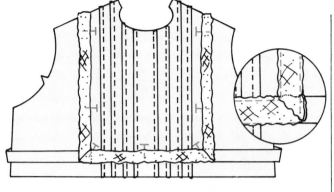

Pin or tape the trim to the front of the dress starting at one shoulder seam, down to the seam, miter the trim as shown in the illustration, go across ¾'' (2 cm) from the bottom edge, miter the corner and go up to the shoulder. Sew on the trim on both sides. If you wish to have a belt, we suggest that you attach the belt underneath the trim.

SKIRT TUCKS

For a little toddler who is growing very fast, you can make tucks on the bottom of the skirt. The tucks should be large so that they can be removed to lengthen the dress as the child grows. Or you may want to use tucks only for decoration. Be sure to add twice the amount of each tuck to the length of the skirt. When you let out the tucks to lengthen the dress and if you can see the line where the fold was located, you can cover up this line by sewing one or more decorative stitches on the old fold line. You can also sew on a decorative band or rickrack to hide the fold.

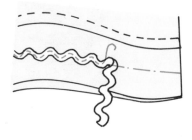

BODICE OVERLAY

The front appearance of a dress can easily be changed with the use of overlay. Use Master Pattern No. 15. If you would like to have a V-front, measure 2'' (5 cm) in from the neck opening on the shoulder. Draw a straight line from this point to the center front, 2½'' (6.5 cm) up from the bottom edge. If you want a square front, measure 2'' (5 cm) in from the neck opening on the shoulder. From the center front on the bottom edge, measure 2½'' (6.5 cm). See illustration. Draw a line from the shoulder to the mark at the bottom of the bodice. Trace the overlay on tissue paper. Add seam allowances to the sides of the overlay.

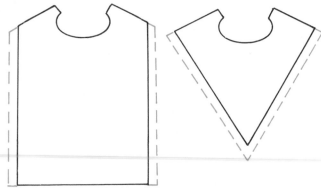

SKIRT AND BLOUSE LOOK   BODICE OVERLAY

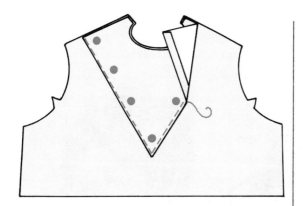

You can use contrasting colors for either the V-front or the square front. Or you may wish to use the same color for the sleeves and the overlay. If you are using a plaid, you can cut the overlay on the bias for a very interesting effect. Place the overlay on top of the front before you start to construct the dress. Fold under the raw edges on each side and topstitch the overlay to the front. You can use either a straight stitch or you may want to use a decorative stitch. Another interesting effect can be obtained with the use of decorative buttons inside the seam on the overlay.

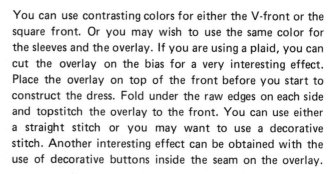

The overlay can be made of the same fabric as the dress with insert lace or eyelet at the seam. Pin the right side of the lace to the right side of the overlay and sew in place. Press the seam to the wrong side with the lace or eyelet extending. Pin the overlay to the bodice front and topstitch close to the edges of the overlay. If you are constructing a square front and you would like to have a tie belt, we recommend that you sew the belt in the seam.

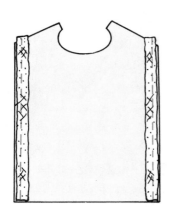

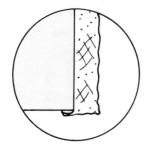

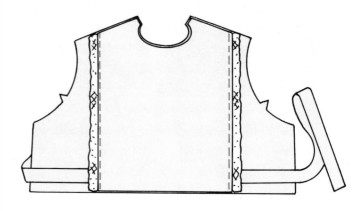

SKIRT AND BLOUSE LOOK: A toddler has difficulty with a skirt and a blouse as the blouse tends to ride up. You can overcome this by making a dress that looks like a blouse and skirt. Use one color fabric for the bodice and another for the skirt. Make suspender straps from the same fabric as the skirt.

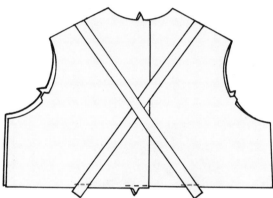

Cut two strips of fabric 2½″ (6.5 cm) wide and the following length:

T1	18″ (46 cm)
T2	18½″ (47 cm)
T3	19″ (48 cm)
T4	19½″ (49.5 cm)

Fold the strips lengthwise, right side to right side. Sew the length of the strap, using a 5/8″ (1.5 cm) seam allowance. Turn the straps right side out. Press the seam in the center of the strap. Sew the straps to the bodice seam, halfway between the center front and the side seams, cross straps in back and attach to the bodice seam.

FAKE TAB

Cut a strip of fabric the length of the bodice from the neckline to the bodice seam at center front. This strip can be the same fabric as used for the top or it can be of a contrasting color.

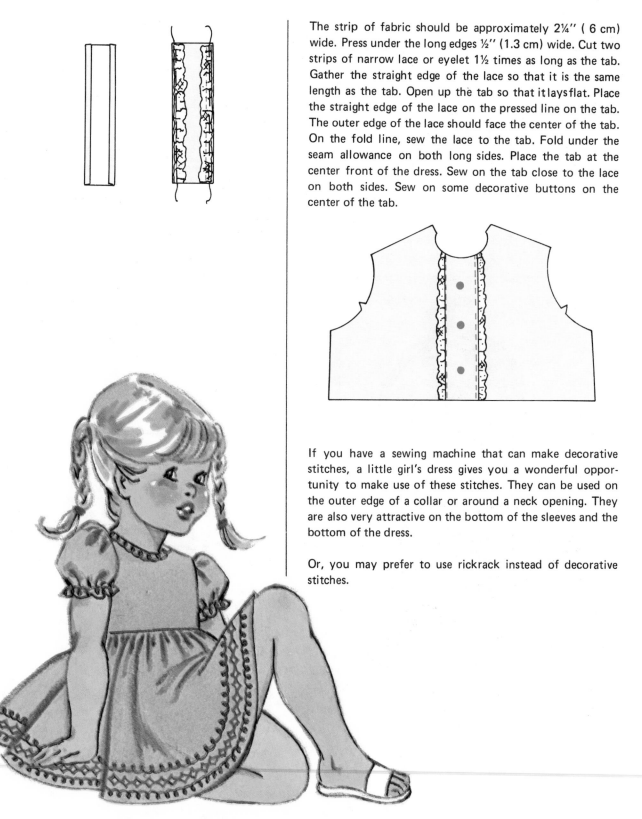

The strip of fabric should be approximately 2¼" (6 cm) wide. Press under the long edges ½" (1.3 cm) wide. Cut two strips of narrow lace or eyelet 1½ times as long as the tab. Gather the straight edge of the lace so that it is the same length as the tab. Open up the tab so that it lays flat. Place the straight edge of the lace on the pressed line on the tab. The outer edge of the lace should face the center of the tab. On the fold line, sew the lace to the tab. Fold under the seam allowance on both long sides. Place the tab at the center front of the dress. Sew on the tab close to the lace on both sides. Sew on some decorative buttons on the center of the tab.

If you have a sewing machine that can make decorative stitches, a little girl's dress gives you a wonderful opportunity to make use of these stitches. They can be used on the outer edge of a collar or around a neck opening. They are also very attractive on the bottom of the sleeves and the bottom of the dress.

Or, you may prefer to use rickrack instead of decorative stitches.

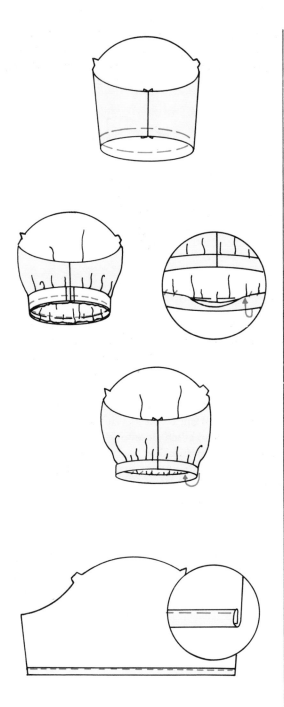

SLEEVES

The bottom of the sleeves may be finished in a variety of ways. One method is to use binding but we only recommend it for short sleeves.

Sew a gathering stitch at the bottom edge of the sleeve. You will need two sleeve bands. Children's arms vary greatly in size. To obtain the correct size, measure around the child's arm and add 1'' (2½ cm) to this measurement. Cut the band 1'' (2.5 cm) wide. Sew the band together to form a circle. Use ¼'' (6 mm) seam allowance.

Place the band, right side to right side, on the sleeve opening with raw edges together. Gather the bottom of the sleeve to fit the band. Sew on the band.

Fold the band over the raw edges to the wrong side. Fold under the raw edges of the band and stitch in place by hand.

If you would like to use bias tape instead of a band, see Section 1 for applying bias tape. If you are using bias tape around the sleeves, it looks very attractive if you also use bias tape around the neck opening.

Another way to finish the bottom of either short or long sleeves is to use elastic. Before you sew the sleeve together, finish the bottom edge of the sleeve either by using a pretty narrow lace or by hemming.

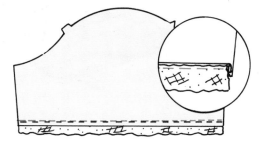

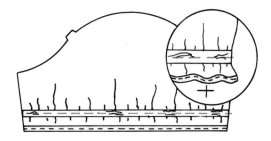

Cut two strips of narrow elastic using the chart given for the basic dress. Place the elastic ¾" (2 cm) up from the bottom edge. Sew on the elastic, stretching the elastic to fit across the sleeve. Now, sew the sleeve seams.

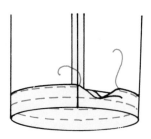

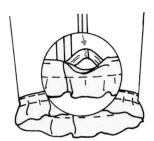

You can make a ruffle with a casing at the bottom of the sleeve by adding twice the width of the ruffle to the length of the bottom edge of the sleeve. We suggest you add 2" (5 cm).

Sew the sleeve seam. Fold up 2 5/8" (6.5 cm) to the wrong side at the bottom of the sleeve. Fold the raw edges under ¼" (6 mm) and stitch close to edge, leaving an opening for inserting the elastic. Sew another seam 3/8" (1 cm) down from the first stitching to make the casing. Thread elastic into the casing. Sew the ends of the elastic together and finish sewing the casing seam.

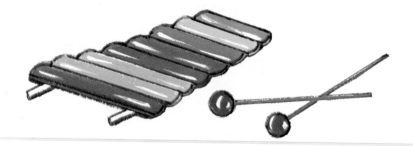

PANTIES

A very attractive outfit may be made by making a pair of panties using the same fabric as the dress or you can use a coordinated color fabric. The fabric should be a lightweight fabric.

Use Master Pattern Nos. 13 and 14. Cut out the pattern pieces and sew the center front and the center back seams. Sew the side seam and then the inside leg seams. The pattern allows a 5/8" (1.5 cm) seam allowance. Sew the seams with a straight stitch. Trim seam allowance to ¼" (6 mm) and overcast the edges together.

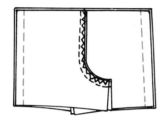

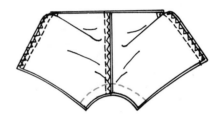

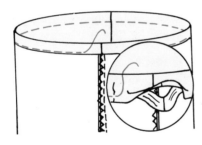

At the waist and at the leg openings, press a 5/8" (1.5 cm) hem to the wrong side. Fold the raw edges under and sew close to the inner edge leaving an opening for inserting the elastic. We recommend that you use a ¼" (6 mm) wide elastic at the waist and the leg openings.

ELASTIC MEASUREMENT CHART

Size	T1	T2	T3	T4
Waist, Cut 1	19" (48 cm)	19½" (49.5 cm)	20" (51 cm)	20½" (52 cm)
Leg Openings, Cut 2	11¼" (28.5 cm)	11½" (29 cm)	11¾" (30 cm)	12" (30.5 cm)

Insert the elastic into the casings. Overlap the ends of the elastic and stitch securely. Close the opening.

A pair of panties can be made to look very pretty by adding rows of lace across the back of the panties. You can either overlap the lace slightly or separate the strips. Sew the center back seam. Mark lines on the right side of the panties where the lace will be applied. You can make as many rows as desired. Use lace approximately ½″ (1.3 cm) wide. Cut the strips of lace 1½ times the width of the back of the panties.

Sew gathering stitches on one edge of the lace. Pin the lace to the panties on the right side, pull the gathering stitches so that the lace fits the fabric. Sew on the lace on top of the gathering stitches. Finish sewing the panties as previously described.

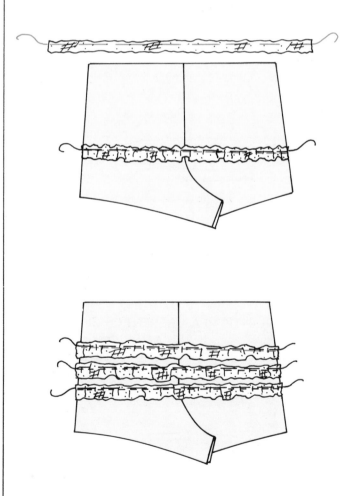

pajamas
and
nightgowns

As many toddlers spend almost half their time in bed, it is very important that pajamas and nightgowns are constructed using a fabric that is soft so that their tender skin is not irritated. We recommend a single knit, either cotton, synthetic or a blend of cotton and synthetic fabric. The fabric should be easy to care for as these garments will be washed repeatedly. At this age, both boys and girls can wear the same style pajamas. The color of the fabric and the type of applique will vary depending upon whether the pajamas are being made for a boy or a girl.

PAJAMAS: Use the Master T-shirt pattern for both boys' and girls' pajama tops. For winter, use the long sleeve T-shirt; for summer, use the short sleeve T-shirt. See Section 2 for instructions on how to make T-shirts.

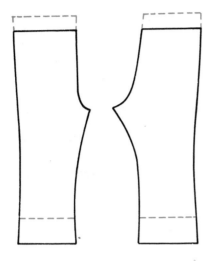

For the pajama bottoms, use Master Pattern No. 1 for the front and Pattern No. 2 for the back. For summer pajamas, you can make short legs.

On both pattern pieces, add 1¾'' (4.5 cm) above the waistline. If you plan to have pajamas with cuffs made from ribbing, shorten the legs 2½'' (6.5 cm) from the bottom. You need two cuffs. You can either buy them ready made or you can make them using ribbing. The ribbing should be 4½'' (11.5 cm) wide and 7½'' (19 cm) long. The ribbing has to be cut across the grain. Remember that when you cut out the pajama pieces, the greatest stretch should go around the body.

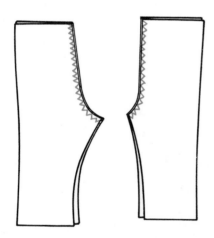

Sew the center front and the center back seam. Sew the inside leg seams and the side seams.

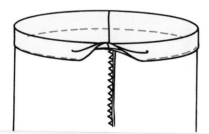

Fold the top edge to the wrong side 1¼'' (3.2 cm). Fold under the raw edges and sew the seam, leaving a 1'' (2.5 cm) opening so that you can insert the elastic.

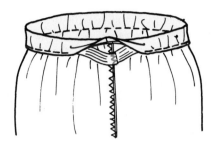

We recommend that you use an elastic that is ¾'' (2 cm) wide. Cut a piece of elastic ½'' (1.3 cm) larger than the waist measurement. Make sure that the elastic is not too tight as children do not feel comfortable if the elastic is too tight. Insert the elastic into the casing. Overlap the ends of the elastic and sew them together. Close the opening.

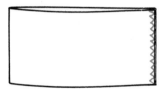

Sew the ends of the cuffs together, right side to right side, to form circles. Fold each cuff double, wrong sides together. Divide the cuffs and the leg openings into half with pins.

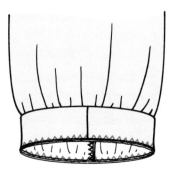

Pin the cuffs to the right side of the leg openings, matching the pins and raw edges. Sew on the cuffs, stretching the cuffs to fit the openings. If you do not plan to use cuffs, simply hem the bottoms of the legs.

PAJAMAS WITH SNAPS AT WAIST

For a small toddler who is still wearing diapers, you may want to use snaps at the waist. When you have made the T-shirt, mark the waistline. Place twill tape on the wrong side of the top at the waistline, topstitch along both sides of the tape. Apply four snaps to the waist of the pajama bottoms, placing the snaps an equal distance from the center front and the center back. Apply snaps on the tape at the waist on the right side of the fabric to match the snaps on the pajama bottoms.

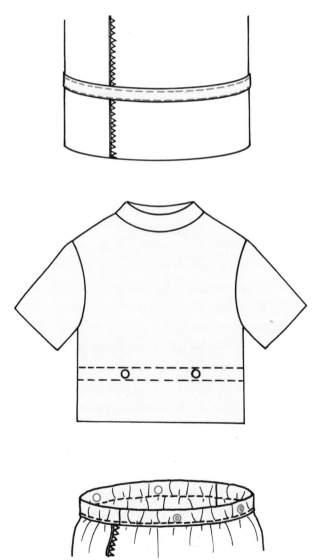

SHORT LEG PAJAMA BOTTOMS WITH LACE

When you are making short leg pajamas for girls, we recommend that you finish the leg openings with elastic and lace.

Sew the side seams. We recommend that you use a narrow lace to finish the leg openings. Overlap the lace on the right side of the leg openings ¼″ (6 mm) and sew close to the inner edge of the lace, using a close zigzag stitch.

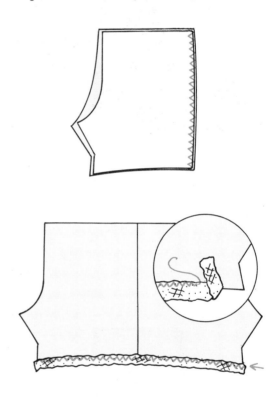

For the elastic, use 1/8″ (3 mm) wide elastic. Measure around the child's legs for the correct length of elastic. The elastic should not be too tight. You need one length of elastic for each leg. If you do not know the measurement for the child, use the following chart.

Size	T1	T2
	10¼″ (26 cm)	10½″ (26.5 cm)
	T3	T4
	10¾″ (27.5 cm)	11″ (28 cm)

Divide the elastic in half with a pin. Divide the leg opening in half with a pin. Place the elastic on the wrong side of the leg opening 1¼'' (3.2 cm) from the edge of the lace. Match the pins and match the ends of the elastic with the ends of the leg opening. Using a zigzag stitch, sew on the elastic, stretching the elastic to fit the leg opening.

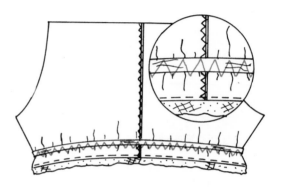

Sew the inside leg seams. Place one leg inside the other leg, right sides together, and sew the crotch seam. Finish the waist with elastic as previously described.

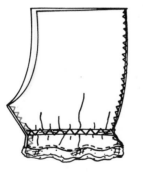

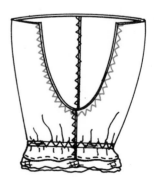

GIRL'S NIGHTSHIRT: You can make a very pretty nightshirt for a little girl using the T-shirt pattern. For the front, use Pattern Piece No. 4; for the back, use No. 5; for the sleeves use No. 3; and for the neckband, use No. 6. The sleeve can be either long or short and they can be finished with either a hem or a cuff.

Adjust the front and back of the pattern pieces by adding the following amount to the length of the T-shirt.

Size	T1	T2
	10" (25.5 cm)	12" (30.5 cm)
	T3	T4
	13½" (34 cm)	15" (38 cm)

You have to flare the sides. You do this by increasing the width of the front and back pattern pieces. At the bottom of the T-shirt pattern, make a mark 1¼" (3 cm) out from the side seams. Draw a straight line through the mark to the bottom edge. See illustration.

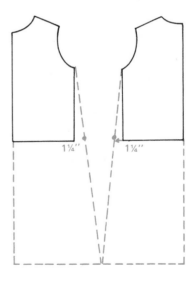

Construct the nightshirt using the same procedures as used for the T-shirt in Section 2.

If you wish to make a nightgown for a little girl, you can use the Master Pattern for a dress and you can make the nightgown any length. The nightgown can be made using any lightweight fabric; both cotton and a cotton blend are very good and for a chilly night, flannel is very nice.

appliques, ideas and gifts

Making appliques is the fun part when you are constructing children's clothes. You can use your imagination to decorate and personalize any outfit or item. Appliques can be applied to both knit and woven fabric. In addition to being fun, they are also easy to make. You can use scrap pieces of fabric for the appliques; these too can be from knit or woven fabric. It is nice to coordinate the applique with the garment. For example, if you are making a T-shirt and pants and you would like to have the applique on the T-shirt, use the pants fabric for the applique. Appliques can be made from one color fabric or you can add other colors of fabric for detail areas. Buttons, metal eyelets, rickrack, narrow ribbons and any trim can be used to add detail to the applique.

We have included some drawings for appliques. These are decorated with various types of trims and buttons.

Draw or copy the applique you wish to use on the fabric. Do not cut out the applique.

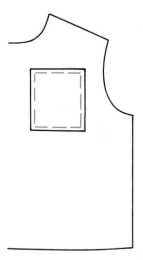

If you are applying the applique to a knit garment, the fabric should be stabilized underneath the applique. Place a piece of lightweight woven fabric or interfacing on the wrong side of the garment under the position of the applique and baste it in place. After the applique is completed, cut off the excess fabric on the wrong side close to the stitches.

Pin the fabric to the garment. Sew around the edges of the design using a narrow zigzag stitch.

Trim away the excess fabric as close as possible to the stitches.

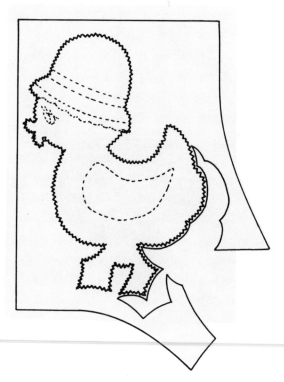

Now sew around the edges of the design again, using a zigzag stitch slightly wider with the stitches closer together. You can create pictures by using different colored fabrics in the same applique.

For a firmer applique, you should stabilize the fabric which will be used for the applique. This procedure will also keep the fabric from unraveling. Use a lightweight press-on interfacing and press it on the wrong side of the fabric to be used for the applique. Cut out the applique.

If you are using an applique with two colors, such as a duck with a hat, first cut out the duck and the hat in the same color as one piece. Cut out the hat using a different color fabric. It is easier to sew on the hat if you fuse the hat to the duck. Use a very small piece of fusible webbing and place it between the duck and the hat. Use a warm iron to attach the hat to the duck. Now fuse the duck to the garment using the same procedure as used for the hat.

Sew on the duck using a very close zigzag stitch over the raw edges. Outline the wing inside the duck. Using a contrasting thread and a wide zigzag stitch, outline the ribbon on the hat. Stitch the eye and the beak. If desired, these small details can be embroidered by hand.

Button

Eyelet

Solid Stitching

Ric Rac

MONOGRAMS

The same techniques as used for applying appliques can be used for monograms and initials. You can also make monograms using bias tape. Cut the pieces of bias tape to be used for the letter. For example, if you are making an E, you will have one long piece of bias tape and three small pieces. Tuck under the edges of the long piece and tape or pin in position. Fold under one end on each of the three small pieces. Tuck the other end of the small piece under the long piece as illustrated. Tape or pin in place and sew a zigzag stitch around all the outer edges.

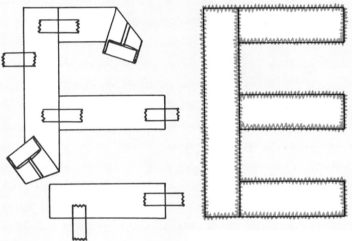

To make a monogram on a sweater, use a piece of yarn in a contrasting color. Start at one end of an initial leaving a few inches of yarn at the beginning. Sew on the yarn using a zigzag stitch. This stitch should be wide enough so that it misses the yarn. Follow the outline of the initial, again leave a piece of extra yarn at the end.

Pull the ends of the yarn to the wrong side and make a knot as close as possible to the fabric. The knots will keep the yarn in place.

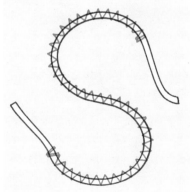

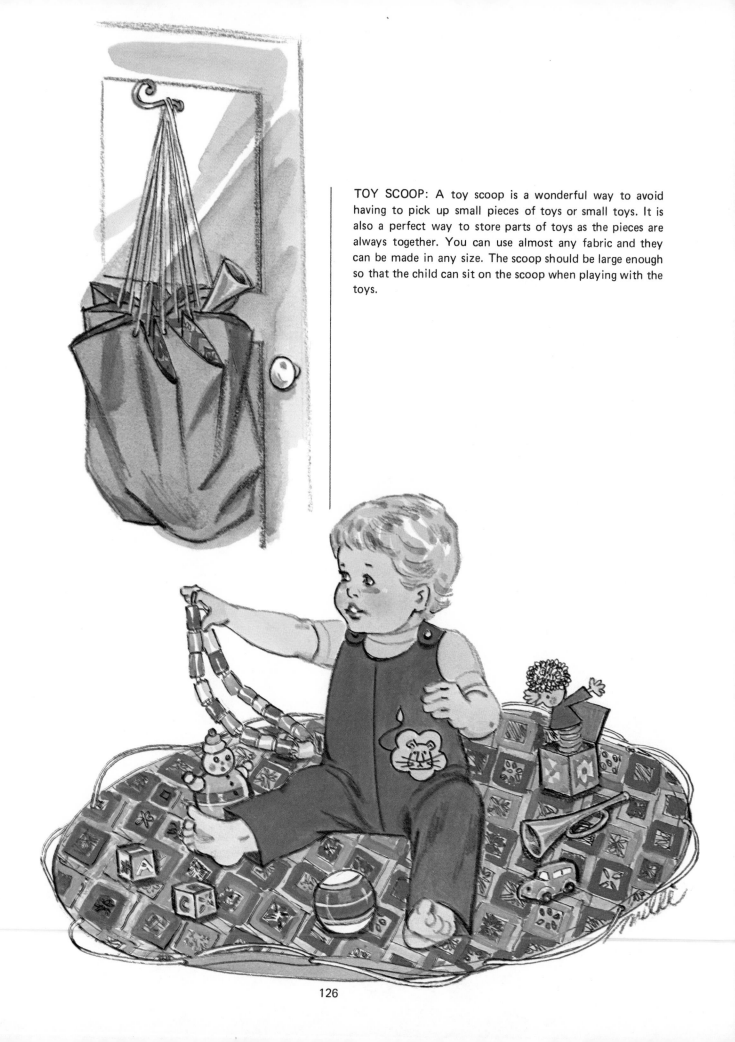

TOY SCOOP: A toy scoop is a wonderful way to avoid having to pick up small pieces of toys or small toys. It is also a perfect way to store parts of toys as the pieces are always together. You can use almost any fabric and they can be made in any size. The scoop should be large enough so that the child can sit on the scoop when playing with the toys.

126

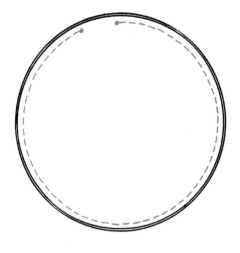

You can use either a single or double layer of fabric. The double layer scoop is easier to construct. Cut out two circles of fabric. Place the fabric, right side to right side, and sew around the circle, leaving an opening large enough to turn the fabric right side out. Close the opening. Sew another seam approximately 1″ (2.5 cm) from the edge around the circle. Apply an even number of metal eyelets an equal distance around the edge of the circle. Thread a cord in and out of the eyelets; make a knot on the ends of the cord. When you want to put the toys away, pick up the cord at four places and you can hang up the toy scoop.

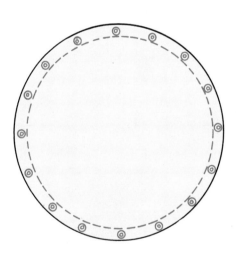

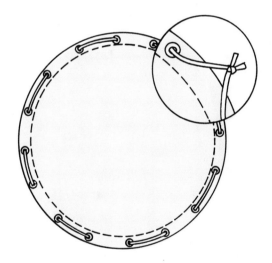

If you are using a single layer of fabric, hem the edges using a 1″ (2.5 cm) hem and proceed as above.

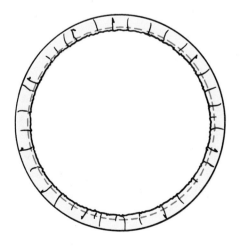

HANDY BAG: If a child attends a nursery school or day care center, they often have to carry items to and from the school or center. A handy bag is perfect for this. Cut a piece of fabric 32" (81 cm) long and 11½" (29 cm) wide. For the handle, cut two pieces 10" (25 cm) long and 2½" (6 cm) wide. Fold the large piece double, wrong side to wrong side to form the bag. Sew a seam on the two long sides using a narrow seam allowance. Turn the bag inside out and sew a seam ¼" (6 mm) from the edge to hide the seam allowance. Turn the bag right side out.

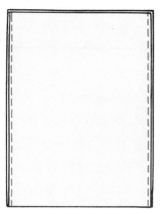

At the top of the bag, fold a 2" (5 cm) hem to the wrong side. Fold under the raw edges and hem. Fold the handle strips, right side to right side, lengthwise. Sew the long side. Turn the strips right side out.

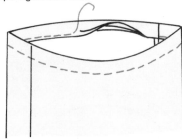

Attach the handles as illustrated to the bag. If you would like to be able to close the top of the bag, sew on a 2½" (6 cm) piece of Velcro on the inside hem between the handles.

If you plan to monogram the bag or to applique it, this should be done before you construct the bag.

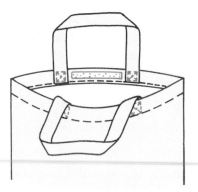

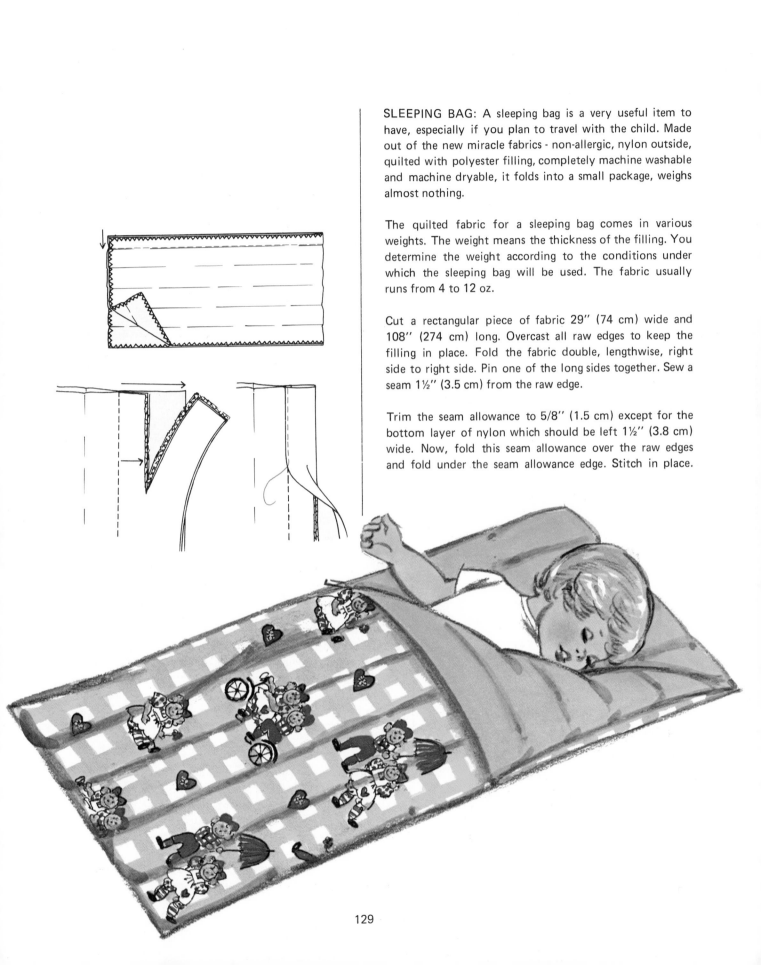

SLEEPING BAG: A sleeping bag is a very useful item to have, especially if you plan to travel with the child. Made out of the new miracle fabrics - non-allergic, nylon outside, quilted with polyester filling, completely machine washable and machine dryable, it folds into a small package, weighs almost nothing.

The quilted fabric for a sleeping bag comes in various weights. The weight means the thickness of the filling. You determine the weight according to the conditions under which the sleeping bag will be used. The fabric usually runs from 4 to 12 oz.

Cut a rectangular piece of fabric 29'' (74 cm) wide and 108'' (274 cm) long. Overcast all raw edges to keep the filling in place. Fold the fabric double, lengthwise, right side to right side. Pin one of the long sides together. Sew a seam 1½'' (3.5 cm) from the raw edge.

Trim the seam allowance to 5/8'' (1.5 cm) except for the bottom layer of nylon which should be left 1½'' (3.8 cm) wide. Now, fold this seam allowance over the raw edges and fold under the seam allowance edge. Stitch in place.

129

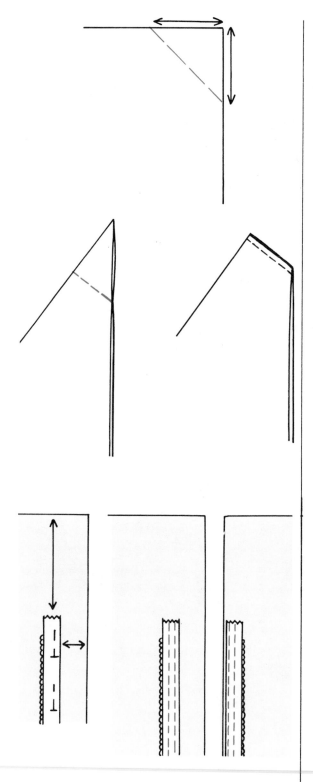

Miter the two corners which will be at the top of the sleeping bag.

To miter the corners, measure 3″ (7.5 cm) from the corners on each side. Mark with pins or chalk. On the wrong side of the fabric, draw a line across from mark to mark.

Fold the corner double, right side to right side, and sew a seam on the line. Trim the excess fabric and turn the corners right side out.

Pin a 1½″ (3.8 cm) hem to the wrong side on the top and to the sides where the opening will be.

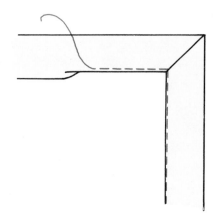

Make sure that you use a heavy zipper, approximately 36″ (91 cm) long.

Place the zipper on the right side of the sleeping bag 12″ (30.5 cm) down from the top edge and 1½″ (3.8 cm) in from the edge. The edge of the zipper tape should face the opening. Be sure that the right side of the zipper is to the right side of the fabric. Pin the zipper in place. The zipper will not go all the way to the bottom of the bag. Sew a seam close to the edge of the zipper tape. Sew a second seam ¼″ (6 mm) in from the first seam. Open the zipper.

Measure the distance from the top of the bag to where the zipper starts. Measure the same distance on the other side. Start pinning the other part of the zipper at this point, right side to right side, with the zipper tape even with the edge of the fabric.

Sew one seam close to the edge of the zipper tape and a second seam ¼″ (6 mm) in from this seam.

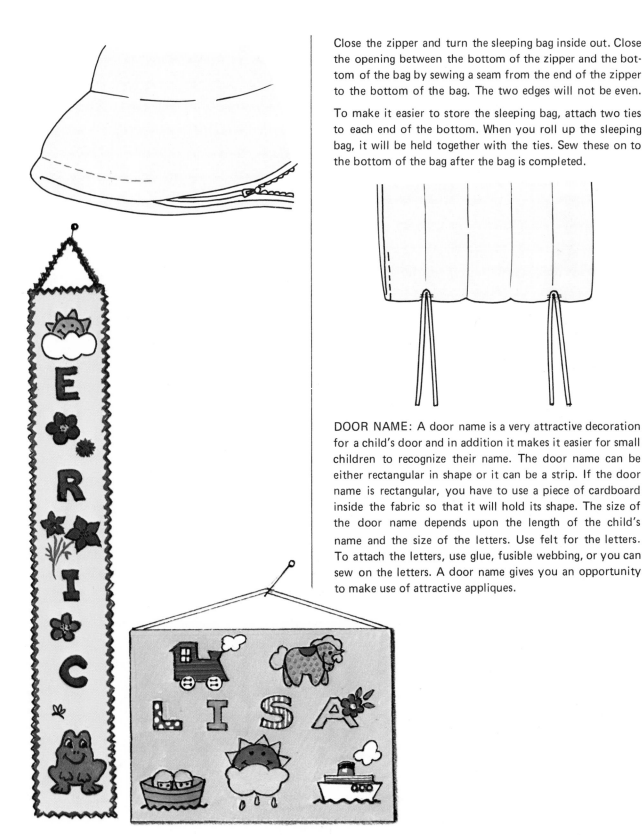

Close the zipper and turn the sleeping bag inside out. Close the opening between the bottom of the zipper and the bottom of the bag by sewing a seam from the end of the zipper to the bottom of the bag. The two edges will not be even.

To make it easier to store the sleeping bag, attach two ties to each end of the bottom. When you roll up the sleeping bag, it will be held together with the ties. Sew these on to the bottom of the bag after the bag is completed.

DOOR NAME: A door name is a very attractive decoration for a child's door and in addition it makes it easier for small children to recognize their name. The door name can be either rectangular in shape or it can be a strip. If the door name is rectangular, you have to use a piece of cardboard inside the fabric so that it will hold its shape. The size of the door name depends upon the length of the child's name and the size of the letters. Use felt for the letters. To attach the letters, use glue, fusible webbing, or you can sew on the letters. A door name gives you an opportunity to make use of attractive appliques.

131

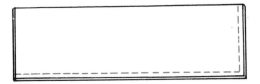

For the strip door name, cut a piece of fabric twice as wide as you wish the finished strip to be. Fold the fabric, lengthwise, right side to right side, and sew the one long side and one short side. Turn the strip right side out. Close the top opening. Sew rickrack around the edge.

Start at the left top corner and go all around the strip. Do not cut off the excess rickrack as this is used to hang the door name. Decide how long you want the rickrack to be and attach it on the right hand corner.

If you are making a rectangular door name, cut two pieces of fabric the same size. Decorate one of the pieces. Place the two pieces, right side to right side, sew the three sides, leaving the top edge open. Turn the fabric right side out. Insert a piece of cardboard and close the top opening. Attach a ribbon or a string at each top corner so that you can hang the door name.

The following pattern pieces are included
in the Master Pattern inside the back cover.

1. Jumpsuit Front
2. Jumpsuit Back
3. T-Shirt Sleeve
4. T-Shirt Front
5. T-Shirt Back
6. T-Shirt Neckband
7. Rugby Tab - Facing
8. Front Tab - Facing for Tab Front
9. Collar - Straight Ends
10. Collar - Rounded
11. Ribbing Cuff - Long Sleeves
12. Rugby Cuff
13. Panties Front - (Dress)
14. Panties Back - (Dress)
15. Dress - Front Bodice

16. Dress - Back Bodice
17. Dress - Sleeve
18. Dress - Collar
19. Overall Front
20. Overall Back
21. Shoulder Strap
22. Bib
23. Waistband
24. Waistband
25. Back Pocket for Pants
26. Lower Pocket (Square Corners)
27. Breast Pocket (Square Corners)
28. Lower Pocket (Rounded)
29. Breast Pocket (Rounded)
30. Short Sleeve Band T-Shirt

YARDAGE REQUIREMENT

Yardage requirements are for basic garments only. Use these only as a guideline for variations of the different garments.

PATTERNS DESIGNED FOR KNIT FABRIC - 60'' (152 cm) Wide

SUGGESTED FABRICS: Single knit (cotton or synthetic), stretch terry, velour. Pants, jumpsuits and coveralls also in double knit, cotton or synthetic.

SIZES	1 and 2	3 and 4		
Jumpsuit-Long Sleeves	1 (0.95)	1 1/8 (1.05)	yd	(m)
Jumpsuit-Short Legs and Sleeves	¾ (0.70)	¾ (0.70)	yd	(m)
Coverall-Long Leg	1 (0.95)	1 1/8 (1.05)	yd	(m)
Coverall-Short Leg	¾ (0.70)	¾ (0.70)	yd	(m)
Pull-on Pants	5/8 (0.60)	¾ (0.70)	yd	(m)
Pull-on Shorts	3/8 (0.35)	3/8 (0.35)	yd	(m)
T-Shirt-RugbyShirt-Tab Front Shirt				
Long or Short Sleeves	½ (0.50)	5/8 (0.60)	yd	(m)
Ribbing for Neckband and Cuffs				
Long Sleeve	¼ (0.25)	3/8 (0.35)	yd	(m)
Short Sleeve	¼ (0.25)	¼ (0.25)	yd	(m)
Rugby Shirt-Contrasting Fabric for				
Collar and Facing	¼ (0.25)	¼ (0.25)	yd	(m)
Open Front Shirt	5/8 (0.60)	5/8 (0.60)	yd	(m)
Pajamas				
Long Leg-Long Sleeve	1 (0.95)	1 (0.95)	yd	(m)
Short Leg-Short Sleeve	¾ (0.35)	7/8 (0.80)	yd	(m)
Ribbing for Neckband and Cuffs for				
Sleeves and Long Legs	3/8 (0.35)	3/8 (0.35)	yd	(m)
Ribbing for Neckband and Sleeve Band	¼ (0.25)	¼ (0.25)	yd	(m)

PATTERNS DESIGNED FOR WOVEN FABRIC - 45'' (115 cm) Wide

SUGGESTED FABRICS FOR DRESS: Lightweight soft or crisp fabrics such as broadcloth, gingham, organdy, eyelet, dotted swiss, batiste.

SUGGESTED FABRICS FOR OVERALLS AND PANTS: Denim, cotton broadcloth, lightweight corduroy, gabardine.

SIZES	1	2	3	4		
Dress-Long Sleeve	1(0.95)	1 1/8(1.05)	1¼ (1.15)	1 3/8(1.30)	yd	(m)
Dress-Short Sleeve	1(0.95)	1 (0.95)	1 1/8(1.05)	1 1/8(1.05)	yd	(m)
Dress with Tiered Skirt						
Long Sleeve	1¼(1.15)	1¼(1.15)	1 3/8 (1.30)	1 3/8 (1.30)	yd	(m)
Short Sleeve	1(0.95)	1(0.95)	1 1/8(1.05)	1 1/8(1.05)	yd	(m)
Panties	3/8 (0.35)	3/8(0.35)	½(0.50)	½(0.50)	yd	(m)
Overalls-Long Leg	7/8(0.80)	1 (0.95)	1(0.95)	1 1/8(1.05)	yd	(m)
Short Leg	5/8(0.60)	¾(0.70)	¾(0.70)	7/8(0.80)	yd	(m)
Bib Front Pants						
Long Legs	¾(0.70)	¾(0.70)	7/8(0.80)	7/8(0.80)	yd	(m)
Short Legs	½(0.50)	5/8(0.60)	5/8(0.60)	¾(0.70)	yd	(m)
Pull-on Pants	¾(0.70)	¾(0.70)	7/8(0.80)	7/8(0.80)	yd	(m)
Pull-on Shorts	3/8(0.35)	½(0.50)	½(0.50)	½(0.50)	yd	(m)

NOTIONS: Notions are not listed. Purchase the notions according to the patterns you are using and the variation you choose to make.